How LIS Professionals Can Use Alerting Services

CHANDOS
INFORMATION PROFESSIONAL SERIES

Series Editor: Ruth Rikowski
(email: Rikowskigr@aol.com)

Chandos' new series of books are aimed at the busy information professional. They have been specially commissioned to provide the reader with an authoritative view of current thinking. They are designed to provide easy-to-read and (most importantly) practical coverage of topics that are of interest to librarians and other information professionals. If you would like a full listing of current and forthcoming titles, please visit our web site **www.chandospublishing.com** or contact Hannah Grace-Williams on email info@chandospublishing.com or telephone number +44 (0) 1865 884447.

New authors: we are always pleased to receive ideas for new titles; if you would like to write a book for Chandos, please contact Dr Glyn Jones on email gjones@chandospublishing.com or telephone number +44 (0) 1865 884447.

Bulk orders: some organisations buy a number of copies of our books. If you are interested in doing this, we would be pleased to discuss a discount. Please contact Hannah Grace-Williams on email info@chandospublishing.com or telephone number +44 (0) 1865 884447.

How LIS Professionals Can Use Alerting Services

INA FOURIE

Chandos Publishing
Oxford • England

Chandos Publishing (Oxford) Limited
Chandos House
5 & 6 Steadys Lane
Stanton Harcourt
Oxford OX29 5RL
UK
Tel: +44 (0) 1865 884447 Fax: +44 (0) 1865 884448
Email: info@chandospublishing.com
www.chandospublishing.com

First published in Great Britain in 2006

ISBN:
1 84334 128 X (paperback)
1 84334 129 8 (hardback)
978 1 84334 128 4 (paperback)
978 1 84334 129 1 (hardback)

British Library Cataloguing-in-Publication Data.
A catalogue record for this book is available from the British Library.

Printed in the UK and USA.

Contents

List of figures and tables

Figure

Tables

Acknowledgements

My appreciation to Chandos Publishing for the opportunity to write this book, as well as to Neill Johnstone for the editing.

Preface

LIS professionals have been aware of the need for current awareness services (CAS) or alerting services over many years, and many use some methods, even if only informal networking, to keep up with developments in their professional fields. Looking at the number of opportunities that have slipped by, however, our efforts do not seem to be quite good enough.

I believe firmly in the potential of information and the difference it can make in our professional lives. I believe in the joy and satisfaction it might bring if information is used creatively at the right time and in the right place to give us a competitive edge. As an educator over many years, I also believe in the potential of people to develop and grow, and to set their own standards for professional achievement.

The World Wide Web has opened so many opportunities for people who have never had access to subject-specific information to keep up with what is happening in their professional fields. The Web puts them in a position to explore new possibilities, and to use their professional talents to exploit new job opportunities and challenges.

I would therefore like to use this book to ask LIS professionals to reconsider the concepts of 'CAS' and 'alerting services' and the ways we can monitor our professional environment. Above all, I would like to use the opportunity to argue that the use of CAS/alerting services is not just a technique and the ability to select useful methods – it also involves our emotions, feelings, enthusiasm and an understanding of our professional world and ourselves in this world.

Technology certainly offers solutions to selecting and filtering information and for dealing with information overload. However, we also need to understand the emotional and intellectual sides of keeping up with developments. We need to understand how we take decisions and how we use information. We need to be critical about our efforts and honest about whether we are doing our best and whether we really are successful. Even if we do not have answers to all the questions, it is still important to acknowledge that it is time to learn more about our information needs and information seeking behaviour, and our efforts to stay abreast.

This book is especially aimed at the possibilities offered by the Web to LIS professionals who do not otherwise have access to information resources such as academic libraries subscribing to services for LIS professionals, subscriptions to professional journals or membership of a selection of professional bodies.

I was very excited when initially proposing the title and signing the contract with Chandos Publishing in 2004, and when thinking of what I would like to achieve with the book. I am still excited, but more acutely aware of how our emotions impact on how we see and experience the world, and our will to put in the extra effort required in keeping up. I am more aware of questions of whether it is worth the effort, but at the same time more aware of the opportunities it may open for each and every LIS professional to claim their stakes in a dynamic world and to use their diversity of talents.

A week after I signed the contract we learned that my husband's leukaemia for which he had been treated since August 2002 had again turned acute. We were still positive that a stem cell transplant would be a cure, and the book seemed like something to keep me going.

I would therefore like to dedicate this book to my husband, David Fourie, who died 24 October 2004 after a stem cell transplant. I started writing the drafts while sitting next to his bed during subsequent heavy dosage treatments of chemotherapy. After his death, it was very difficult to pick up the threads again, and I am grateful to Chandos Publishing for granting an extension on the initial date for submitting the manuscript.

I would also like to dedicate the book to our twin sons, Chris and Herman, who were at the beginning of their final year school exams when David died. They successfully completed their exams and finished their first year at university. I admire their courage to see things through.

Life is precious: we need to share our lives with loved ones, but we should also use our abilities to exploit opportunities coming our way, and to seek fulfilment in our jobs.

Ina Fourie
Pretoria
May 2006

About the author

Dr Ina Fourie is an associate professor at the Department of Information Science, University of Pretoria, South Africa. She joined the Department in 2001 when leaving the University of South Africa (Unisa – a distance teaching university) where she had been a lecturer and senior lecturer since 1988.

Ina started her career at the Library and Information Service of the Atomic Energy Corporation of South Africa where she was responsible for preparing the South African input on nuclear energy and related fields for the International Nuclear Information System. The topic for her doctorate dealt with the design of a multimedia study package for distance teaching in information retrieval. She also holds a postgraduate diploma in tertiary education.

Ina's research interests include, among other things, information behaviour, collaborative information seeking, distance and telematic teaching, current awareness/alerting services, instructional design, aspects of information organisation, professional development, and information literacy. She is currently doing research with Retha Claasen-Veldsman on the information needs of oncology health care professionals and especially their need for current awareness/alerting services. They intend to expand the project to cater for the information needs of cancer patients.

Ina has two sons, Chris and Herman, who are 19 and in their second year at university. She likes to read, travel, and prepare international dishes. Short local holiday breaks and visiting South African wine vineyards (picnics are always a priority) are also a favourite.

The author may be contacted at the following:

Professor Ina Fourie
Department of Information Science
IT Building 6–65
University of Pretoria
Lynnwood Road
Pretoria 0002
South Africa

E-mail: *ina.fourie@up.ac.za*
Tel: +27 12 420-5216
Fax: +27 12 362-5181

Introduction

When starting my career in 1983 at the Library and Information Service (LIS) of the Atomic Energy Corporation of South Africa, I became aware of how important it is for scientists and researchers to keep up with the latest developments in their fields. At the time, there was much concern about the increasing growth in publications and how difficult it was to keep up. The library and information science literature also argued for LIS to provide current awareness services (CAS) to their users. There were many publications on the benefits of CAS, how to run CAS, the choice of methods for CAS, and especially on the value of using computers for CAS. Although the term 'alerting services' was sometimes used instead of CAS, CAS seemed to be the term preferred by the textbooks of the time, such as Kemp (1979) and review articles such as that by Wente and Young (1970). The term 'selective dissemination of information' (SDI) or 'dissemination of information' was also sometimes used (Whitehall, 1982). For this introduction, however, I would prefer to use the term 'CAS'.

Although the Corporation was offering CAS to the scientists and researchers, as was the case in many other scientific and research organisations, it did not seem to specifically encourage the use of such services by LIS professionals. Unlike the researchers and scientists, the LIS professionals were not subscribing to expensive, commercial SDI profiles, which were run on a regular basis against electronic databases available through online services such as Dialog. There were no lists of new books on LIS topics, or LIS related journals being circulated. In fact, it is hard to imagine a specialised library or information service budgeting for LIS books, journal subscriptions, conference attendance, and so on at the same level as for their core business, such as research in the nuclear field, gold mining or car manufacturing. It is even harder to imagine LIS professionals working in school and public libraries having the benefit of CAS at the same level as for researchers and scientists. LIS professionals in academic libraries may perhaps be in a slightly better position, especially if they have an academic LIS department and can share in the CAS offered to that department. If employers do not offer opportunities to use CAS, LIS professionals, however, have to rely on their own resources. There are many who are privileged enough to subscribe to commercial CAS, to be members of professional organisations and to attend conferences. There are, however, even more LIS professionals who do not have access to these opportunities, and who need to explore other possibilities.

To justify the cost of CAS, organisations had to show an increase in productivity, research output and competitiveness. Although these were never strictly monitored (Williams (1988) is one of the exemptions) it was generally believed that effective CAS could make a useful contribution.

In the LIS literature, many arguments on offering users CAS, or the alternative, alerting services, have been put forward. LIS professionals have used these arguments to promote CAS for scientists, researchers, businessmen and sometimes academics. Despite this, they have somehow failed to make a convincing case for developing their own culture of current awareness or convincing management to spend significant amounts on such services for their own benefit.

An exception is NewsAgent, the alerting service for LIS professionals, discussed by Yeates (1999) and a number of co-workers (e.g. Tedd and Yeates, 1998) and more recent services such as the Informed Librarian. Even so, NewsAgent has now been discontinued, due to lack of funding to keep the project going.

Given that CAS have been around for many years, it might well be assumed that LIS professionals are now sufficiently familiar with them that the topic needs no further exploration. We understand the methods and the reasons for CAS. We are using these methods and all we now require are the technological solutions for information filtering and on how to avoid information overload. This would make this book redundant. But if we are so clued-up at using CAS, why do we often end up being too late to seize the right opportunities, and getting our planning in place for new developments?

In 1988, Stenstrom and Tegler expressed concern about how LIS professionals were using CAS. Wilson (1993) also makes it clear that 'keeping current' does not necessarily imply a change of knowledge. Although I do not want to create the impression that LIS professionals are not using CAS, I share Stenstrom and Tegler's concern: we might need to reconsider *how* we are keeping up, and whether we are really making the best of our possibilities. With all our knowledge and expertise, I would expect our CAS culture to be *much* stronger by now and much more of an example to professionals from other fields.

The intention of this book is not to propagate CAS (or alerting services as it would be called in this book) as something LIS professionals have never heard of, as this is certainly not the case. Indeed, many LIS professionals are using at least one service or method to keep up to date.

This book hopes to widen our concept of CAS and to link the use of CAS to our understanding of information seeking behaviour, and creativity and knowledge generation. I believe that to exploit the power of CAS fully, we need to know much more about ourselves. We need to acknowledge the complexities of information needs and putting information to use. This will never be easy. We also need to realise that we need to learn a lot more about our options, and the choices we make. We especially need to understand how this can impact on how well we understand the field in which we are working, and how we are using the opportunities that come our way.

A decade or two ago it *might* have been possible to argue that LIS work could not justify the costs involved in commercial CAS, and that developments in the field were rather slow. In addition, it might not always be clear how a company or organisation can benefit from new developments in the LIS field. In our current, dynamic environment it seems difficult for LIS professionals not to show off their personal strategies to stay abreast of their field, and to be surrounded by an aura of 'we are the best at current awareness', 'we are alert and we are doing something about it'. 'We are proud to be LIS professionals with very special skills'. There are so many things happening in the LIS world that can make a difference that we can no longer afford not to take note and react. There is also so much information available for free, that we no longer have excuses for not being on top of things. The Web has taken away most of our excuses. The time and effort required to stay on top of things can still be offered as valid arguments, but we will address this later on.

In 1999, I completed an excellent online course on the Internet and CAS, offered by the Faculty of Information Science at the University of Toronto. The course was developed by Gwen Harris and Sandra Wood. It made me realise how much information is freely available to LIS professionals, as well as other users of the Internet. Some ideas on these are shared in two earlier articles on empowering end-users to use CAS, and CAS for acquisitions librarians (Fourie 1999a, 2003a). Since then, even more opportunities have become available, and there is even more pressure on LIS professionals to hold their own in their subject field and careers.

As an educator, I became more aware of the concerns about disintermediation (Fourie 1999b), and the survival of the LIS profession (Fourie, 2004). With each article or book I read, or conference I attend, I realise just how much pressure there is on LIS professionals to keep up, but also how many wonderful opportunities there are if we fully exploit, reconsider and enhance the skills and knowledge we have refined over many decades in the information profession. It is time to draw on everything we have, and to take a fresh approach to survive in the twenty-first century. We should not, however, just merely survive; LIS professionals need to thrive and set the tone in staying abreast of developments. We should be a benchmark for other professions. We should use alertness to make a difference. However, this is easier said than done. This is also something I learned while writing this book. I feel so strongly about the opportunities we may have if we are alert to our professional environment and the personal joy and satisfaction that it might bring, that I tend to forget that we are human beings who get tired, frustrated and anxious about whether we are on the right road, and whether our efforts are worthwhile.

The terms 'current awareness services' (CAS) and 'alerting services' are often used interchangeably. Although the term CAS has been used in this introduction as it was used in the early textbook literature, this book will in fact use 'alerting services', because it seems to fit in better with the intention of professional survival and the use of alerting services to seize opportunities – which will be the focus of this book. Arguments on the use of terminology will be pursued in more detail in Chapter 2. Both terms are, however, extensively used in the subject literature.

Against the background of a rapidly changing and dynamic environment, this book will explore the potential of alerting services to help LIS professionals to enhance their professional development and to ensure a position in the roles they find exciting. It will focus on taking note of information, turning information into knowledge and using information in a creative and innovative manner. In order to do so, I will draw on the literature of current awareness services/alerting services, environmental scanning, LIS professional development, forecasting, learning theories, information behaviour, creativity, career planning, time management, and so on.

More specifically the book will explore:

- the concept of alerting services and what we hope to achieve;

- insights from other fields and professions to ensure professional development, and alertness (e.g. the use of environmental scanning techniques);

- how changes in the environment may affect LIS professionals in practice as well as LIS educators, and the benefits of monitoring such changes through alerting services and environmental scanning;

- the need for LIS professionals to offer a benchmark to others in the use of alerting services;

- the variety of alerting services that might be useful for LIS professionals (practitioners and educators), with special reference to Web services, and how information gained can be applied in a variety of scenarios;

- the need for LIS professionals to understand and adapt their information behaviour and use of alerting services within the context of information behaviour studies. An innovative look will be taken at this, to move beyond the reasons normally advanced for the use of CAS;

- suggestions to cope with the negative side of alerting services (e.g. information overload);

- pragmatic advice on optimising information gained from alerting services in order to make a difference, and using information to support knowledge generation and creativity.

The following chapters will discuss how LIS professionals can use alerting services in combination with other methods to survive in their professional environment. The emphasis will be on learning from what we know about alerting services and survival, but also on asking that we take a critical look at our traditional assumptions and beliefs – and that we reconsider them.

Although very serious matters, I think the best way to cope with our challenges is to find joy and inspiration in doing all the hard work of staying alert and thinking about the implications, and to accept the fact that there are no ultimate recipes for survival. There is no one single and perfect solution, action or method. There are no perfect decisions, and there is never just one way of interpreting challenges. Even our best efforts will be challenged in the near future, but by working on our survival skills on a daily basis we will become 'fitter' and it will be easier to cope. According to Whitehall (1982: 357) successful CAS can even contribute to a habit of gathering and using information. It seems that it should be the most natural thing for LIS professionals to have such habits by now. We may, however, also realise that we have been monitoring the wrong things

– our efforts to be alert have not gained us anything: 'Or one may be interested in a field of activity where nothing is happening – one stays current by continuing to look for something to happen, but nothing does … Current does not mean better' (Wilson, 1993).

Furthermore, simply reading and noticing does not necessarily mean that one's knowledge will change. Using one or more services to stay abreast does not *per se* mean that you understand your environment. Noting everything that might be potentially worthwhile in your professional environment does not guarantee that you will make the right choices.

To help us in becoming alert to our professional challenges, and to work on putting information to use, the following chapters will be covered:

- Chapter 2: evolution of the concepts of current awareness services, alerting services, environmental scanning, and an expanded perception of alerting services and being alert.

- Chapter 3: how changes in the environment may affect LIS professionals in practice as well as LIS educators, and the benefits of monitoring such changes through alerting services. The need for LIS professionals to offer a benchmark to others in the use of alerting services will also be considered.

- Chapter 4: the variety of alerting services that might be useful for LIS professionals (practitioners and educators), with special reference to Web services, and how information gained can be applied in a variety of scenarios.

- Chapter 5: the need for LIS professionals to understand and adapt their information behaviour and use of alerting services within the context of information behaviour studies. An innovative look will be taken at this in order to move us beyond the standard guidelines for alerting services.

- Chapter 6: possibilities for coping with the negative side of alerting services (e.g. information overload).

- Chapter 7: insights from other fields and professions to ensure professional development, and alertness. Pragmatic advice will be offered on optimising information gained from alerting services in order to make a difference, and using information to support knowledge generation and creativity.

The more one reads and thinks about this, the more it seems impossible to find a solution to be highly alert and proactive. However, if we take a few steps in this direction it will become easier and easier, and once we realise how exciting it can be to explore the options for being alert, and put information to use, our professional lives can become fun and stimulating. A good sense of humour can take one a long way. Barbara Quint (2005), editor of *Searcher Magazine*, and certainly an excellent role model to LIS professionals in terms of alertness, takes a tongue-in-cheek approach in sharing her views on new developments and the role of intermediaries with readers:

> Imagine yourselves back at the dawn of time – library time, I mean. There you stand, an invisible presence, at the bent shoulder of some becowled monk who suddenly straightens up and breaks his vow of silence with the loud proclamation, 'Hey! I already illuminated a manuscript that looks just like this. Why the @#$@#$ doesn't someone catalog this stuff so we don't have to keep making these (bleepedy-bleep) mistakes?' Or let us whisk forward to a chemical laboratory just a century or

more ago. There stands a chemist taking off his lab coat and reaching for his muffler and galoshes. We hear him say, 'I don't care how much work we have to do yet. Even if that lab rat we call our manager fires me for it, I'm going to the ACS meeting and telling them that if they want to keep getting my dues, they've got to find a way to track all these articles every chemist with a pencil keeps writing day and night!

But let's be pragmatic: it is also scary to deal with all the new things we are noting and need to learn about. It is even more scary, to know that we have to do something about them. This book hopes to make it a little bit easier to take the first steps in this direction. But even 'easier' can be challenging and tiring. Perhaps this book should be sold with a supply of vitamin supplements and energy boosters! On the other hand, one should also note the observation by Wilson (1993): '... but even where there is a lot to do, it can happen that thin and superficial information works well enough, the cost of ignorance turns out not to be too great, and, if necessary, bluffing works nicely'. Why then spend a lot of time and effort to be alert, if you can get by without it? If this is true – and I believe it might often be the case – then why bother with alerting services?

As an academic I am tempted to quote substantially from the subject literature, to prove that I have read the literature, to support all the arguments and to show that I know what is happening in the field. A definitive effort was, however, made in this book to limit references to the essential – even so, the list of core references at the end of the book is fairly substantial. These can also be consulted for more references to the subject literature.

I hope that this book will encourage LIS professionals to take up the challenge of being alert on a wider scale than before and with different intentions. I hope that they will realise that it is not such an impossible and daunting task. At the same time, however, I am scared that the reader will think that I am totally naïve in underestimating the complexities of information seeking, information needs, creativity and knowledge generation. I am not: I merely think it is time to explore our full potential as clued-up LIS professionals, and if at the same time we can be encouraged to delve deeper into the complexities of our own behaviour, and getting involved in studies on information seeking behaviour it would really be a bonus. (My own alerting service concerns information seeking and information needs and especially collaborative information seeking and learning.)

I support the idea that technological solutions may take us a long way in staying alert and dealing with information overload, but there is more to the effective use of alerting services. Remember we are not just using these services to know what is happening: we are using them to professionally survive! While writing the book, I realised just how hard I still need to work on my own alertness, and how inadequate my own efforts are in making a difference and in 'surviving'.

2

'Current awareness' or 'alerting' services: where do we come from and where are we heading?

Introduction

The terms 'current awareness services' (CAS) and 'alerting services' both appear in the early LIS literature. CAS seems to be preferred in the early textbooks and review articles, although the term 'alerting services' is also often mentioned in the early journal literature. It sometimes seems as if it does not make a difference which term we use, or how we interpret it – in the end it is about noting new information and keeping up with a field of interest or specialisation. As explained in the introductory chapter, CAS or alerting services have been around for many years – and surely LIS professionals understand the concept by now. I believe that our understanding of concepts may, however, have an impact on how we use something or what we expect from it. Our understanding of concepts often changes over time – for example, the concept of libraries has moved from focusing on books to a variety of multimedia. Sometimes it might also be necessary to make a definite effort to change our understanding – which is what I hope to do in this chapter.

From complaints about opportunities and new roles missed by LIS professionals, it seems as if we are not always successful in what we do (Finlay and Finlay, 1996; Fourie, 2004). We live in very dynamic, changing and challenging professional worlds. Our situations are constantly changing. So may the meaning of concepts. As explained in the introductory chapter, alerting services are not just about noting new information, such as new terms, but also about challenging and changing our interpretations and applications of information. Perhaps it is time to reconsider our interpretation of 'alerting services' and 'being alert'.

I believe that it might make a difference if we reconsider our reasons for monitoring developments in our professional environment, as well as what we hope to achieve by doing so. I would, therefore like to take a bit of the reader's time in going back to our roots for CAS and alerting services. Understanding where we come from might help us to reconsider the concepts we are talking about and to figure out where we need to go.

I will first look at the concepts of 'CAS' and 'alerting services'. Early developments and the traditional rationale for offering these services will be considered, before I explain why it is necessary to move to the terms 'alerting services' and 'being alert' within the context of this book. Before explaining the 'expanded' interpretation of alerting services, I will also look at the concept of 'environmental scanning' and then the differentiation between CAS/alerting services and retrospective searching.

Other terms that are found in the subject literature are 'alerts', and 'current alerting services – individual article supply' (Davies, Boyle and Osborne, 1998). The latter was coined because of LIS users' need to link CAS to document supply services: they do not just want to take note of information, they also want the information immediately at hand. These terms will not, however, be analysed in more detail.

In the following sections, I will look at the early interpretations of CAS and alerting services, as well as at environmental scanning.

Early current awareness services

CAS have been offered by LIS for many years. As early as 1945, H. P. Luhn made his first reference to using computers for CAS, and Martha Williams (1978) proclaimed the need for LIS to offer CAS to users and to help them to develop personal databases to organise and manage the information collected through CAS and retrospective searches.

The methods for early CAS, which we can also regard as traditional CAS, are well documented. Good examples are Behrens (1989), Hamilton (1995), Kemp (1979), Rowley (1985, 1994, 1998) and Whitehall (1982, 1985). Several editions of the *Handbook of Special Librarianship and Information Work* have also included contributions on CAS or the dissemination of information, namely Richards (1992), Trench (1997) and Whitehall (1982). Fourie (2001) added to this in the eighth edition of the *Handbook of Information Management*. Several review articles on CAS have also appeared in the *Annual Review of Information Science and Technology* (e.g. Housman, 1973; Landau, 1969; and Wente and Young, 1970). Electronic CAS methods have also received attention. Electronic tables of content, for example, have been discussed by Cox and Hanson (1992), Davies, Boyle and Osborne (1998), Deardorff and Garrison (1997), Hanson and Cox (1993), Hentz (1996) and Mountifield (1995). Van Brakel and Potgieter (1997) consider the use of Web-based bulletin boards to enhance CAS.

Although we need to note the methods and will do so at a later stage, it is more important to first understand the concept of and the rationale behind offering CAS.

CAS was introduced by LIS for a specific purpose and with a specific understanding of what it should achieve. The reason why it is considered here is that many LIS professionals 'grew up' with this perception of what CAS is, and especially with what it should achieve. Many of us started our careers with the traditional methods of CAS, such as acquisitions lists, indexing and abstracting bulletins, internal bulletins, newspaper clippings, personal notes or phone calls from other LIS professionals, the circulation of the latest editions of journals or photocopies of the tables of contents, or a display shelf with the latest books added to the collection. One type of CAS that was especially important in the use of electronic information services was selective dissemination of information (SDI – a term that is sometimes used interchangeably with alerting services). Some databases used for SDI are updated on a daily basis, while others are updated only every month. (Many other methods for CAS have also been discussed in the subject literature, but will not be considered here.)

Gradually CAS were also made available on CD-ROM databases and through other electronic methods, until we get to the variety of modern CAS available through the Web that forces us to reconsider the concept, purpose and expectations of CAS. Web CAS are discussed by Fourie (1999a), Gustitus (1998), Klingerer (1997), Makulowich (1997), and Ojala (1997) among others. More recent publications include Anderson (2003), Martin and Metcalfe (2001) and Sullivan (2004). What is interesting about the Web-based CAS is that many services are available for free or at a modest fee. There are, however, also services that are very expensive and certainly aimed at the corporate market, such as the British Library's Inside (*http: //www.bl.uk/services/ current/inside.html*).

LIS professionals are certainly aware of these services. The question, however, is whether we are fully exploiting them and whether we have adapted our perceptions of what we hope to achieve. As more information is easily accessible through the Web than in the days of early CAS, we can also expect to monitor a much wider spectrum of developments in our environment – if we wish to, and if we consider it to be necessary.

Current awareness used to mean being aware of what is currently being published as soon as it is made available, in other words, taking note of information as soon as it becomes available. Indeed, the term 'current awareness' was coined to describe the state of keeping up with new developments. It was argued that this can give one a competitive edge, especially if information is monitored against a profile of the users' interests. The 'profile' is similar to a search strategy. The emphasis was on *noting* new information – that is, information that you were not aware of before.

A CAS was seen as an ongoing service that enables one to monitor new information on a regular basis, with regard to a specific topic requiring such monitoring. In the research environment especially, there was a need for people to note new research findings and projects that would stimulate or contradict their own research, or point them in a different, more productive direction. In addition to factual information and all information published during a specific period, LIS users sometimes also need to take note of the latest information on an ongoing basis. CAS offer such information.

At the time, the competitive edge laid in access to information and the ability to afford such access. The focus was also strongly on specific work-related information, such as research findings, business statistics, news reports, and new products. Although the interpretation of information was always important, it is much more so now, as a much larger part of the population has access to information for free via the Web. It is no longer good enough to impress at conferences and cocktail parties with a few off-the-cuff remarks about new developments to give the impression that you know what is going on in the world around you. Success will lie in the very timely use of information. As Choo (2002: xiii) explains in his book *Information Management for the Intelligent Organization*: 'Competition is the consequence of the unequal distribution of information among organizations and their differential abilities to acquire, absorb, and act on information'.

There are many formal definitions of CAS in the early CAS literature. The following are worth consideration:

> For reviewing newly available documents, selecting items relevant to needs of an individual or group, and recording them so that notifications may be sent to those individuals or groups to whose needs they are related. (Kemp, 1979: 12)

> A system, and often a publication, for notifying current documents to users of libraries and information services, e.g. selective dissemination of information, bulletin, indexing service, current literature. (Prytherch, 1995)

> ... a service which provides the recipient with information on the latest developments within the subject areas in which he or she has a specific interest or need to know. (Hamilton, 1995)

According to these definitions a CAS:

- could be a system (e.g. a database), service (e.g. news clippings) or a publication (e.g. acquisitions list or indexing or abstracting bulletin);

- notifies users about current documents (e.g. books, reports, standards, journal articles);

- provides users with information on the latest subject developments;

- allows users to specify the subject areas in which they are interested or need to know about developments.

To allow for the wider variety of CAS that became available via the Web, Fourie redefined CAS as:

> a selection of one or more systems that provide notification of the existence of new entities added to the system's database or of which the system took note (e.g. documents, websites, events such as conferences, discussion groups, editions of newsletters). CAS automatically notify users or allow users to check periodically for updates. The entities can be specified according to users' subject interests or according to the type of entity (e.g. books or newsletters). (Fourie, 1999a: 382)

This definition brings the following to the fore:

- It might be necessary to use more than one system (as will be pointed out, this is probably advisable). Rowley (1998), for example, remarks: 'Many of these developments herald a very much enhanced availability of current information and users may keep themselves reasonably aware of developments by selecting an appropriate range of authoritative sources and scanning these on a regular basis'. Note the reference to scanning; there is no mentioning of taking action.

- The system can be a traditional database (e.g. the Dialog databases or a search engine).

- Users are notified about the existence of new entities, which may include books, journal articles, newsletters, websites, research reports, videos, discussion groups, conference calls for papers, etc.

- Although some systems automatically notify users, it might sometimes be necessary to check sporadically for new updates/new information.

- Different approaches can be followed in monitoring the new information (e.g. according to subject interest or according to the type of entity, such as books on oncology nursing, new books by Isabel Alende, or new CDs by Bryan Adams).

It needs to be pointed out that in all of these definitions we worked from our early perceptions of current awareness and what CAS should offer LIS users. In the early days (before the Web) access to information often gave a competitive advantage; such access was often expensive, and required special skills to identify the information. LIS professionals used such skills to offer CAS to their users. CAS was about *taking note* of new information. Furthermore, it seemed as if the emphasis was on the use of such services by professionals from a variety of fields and how LIS professionals were offering such services to them (e.g. Anderson; 2003; Brunshill, 1997; Gessesse, 1998). There is hardly any research or discussions on LIS professionals using CAS for their own purposes. Exceptions include discussions by Stenstrom and Tegler (1988), Tedd and Yeates (1998) and Yeates (1999). As I will also point out later in this book, extensive research is therefore required about how LIS professionals use CAS, and how we put the information to use. Understanding our own actions should enhance our understanding of users' information behaviour and our ability to exploit the full potential of the Web to empower the wider society in terms of information literacy.

I have used the term 'current awareness services' in a number of early publications (Fourie 1999a, 2001, 2003a), and also in a recent conference paper on CAS for oncology nurses (Fourie and Claasen-Veldsman, 2005). I have argued that little has really changed from the earlier current awareness services in terms of what is being offered and the rationale for using these services. Why use a new term when the emphasis is still on becoming aware of the existence of new information – in other words if the emphasis is still only on noting work or subject related information? Considering the need for LIS professionals to actually take action when noting new information if they wish to survive in their current day environment, it seems appropriate to reconsider the difference between CAS and alerting services, and what we understand or should understand by alerting services and being alert.

Early alerting services

The term 'alerting services' was already used in the very early LIS literature (e.g. Bottle, 1973; Woodburn, 1972). A search of *Information Science and Technology Abstracts* also reveals references to alerting services dating back to 1968. It is therefore certainly not a new concept in the LIS literature. The connotation of the term was very similar to the explanation of CAS and it was often used as a synonym for SDI services. With the introduction of Web services, a number of database or aggregator services started to use the term 'alerts' or 'alerting services' more actively, taking note of new information, as well as simply noting it.

Moving on to a reinterpretation of alerting services, what can we learn from environmental scanning?

Environmental scanning

The term 'environmental scanning' was first coined by Aguilar in 1967 (Choo, 2002). It is mostly associated with organisations and especially learning organisations. It can, however, also be used by professions or a group of organisations as in the OCLC *Environmental Scanning Report* (2003). Non-profit organisations, such as schools, have also shown interest in environmental scanning (e.g. Holmes, McElwee and Thomas, 1995). In the following paragraphs I will consider what we can learn from environmental scanning to expand our concept of alerting services and being alert, as environmental scanning seems to be aimed at favourably positioning organisations. According to Karim (2004), having skills in environmental scanning will certainly also make LIS professionals more marketable.

Environmental scanning enables us to get a holistic picture of developments in the wider, external environment that may have an impact on, say, the organisation or profession. It is based on information needs and includes information seeking, information gathering, and the interpretation and use of information. (The interpretation and use of information is especially important – this moves us beyond merely being aware of information.) Apart from the external environment, it can also cover the internal environment – what is happening inside an organisation. Environmental scanning is often justified by the need to monitor the external and internal environment in order to survive: we need to secure and improve our positions (Wei and Lee, 2004). It can also help us to keep a competitive edge, to identify threats and to avoid surprises – certainly all things that LIS professionals can benefit from!

A discussion by Abels (2002) highlights some points worth considering if we intend to expand our concept of alerting services to allow for the benefits that can be gained from environmental scanning:

- Environmental scanning can be done on different levels of depth and breadth. The level of scanning will, among other things, depend on how important environmental scanning is for our success and survival. This can be linked to levels of uncertainty or anxiety about what the environment might hold that will affect our future. According to Abels (2002) 'The relationship between an organisation and its environment depends upon the internal strengths and weaknesses of the company, which means that an opportunity for one company will be viewed as a threat to another company, depending on how well each is positioned to deal with the specific trend or issue'. This is also very true of individuals and their efforts to keep up with developments, and to put information to use.

- Environmental scanning can help us to identify our strengths and weaknesses.

- Typical aspects to monitor include: competition, technology, economics, regulations, social conditions, trends, events, relationships, change, patterns and forces. When identifying competition, however, one should look beyond the obvious competitors. Libraries have always considered information brokers as competitors. Now however, they, also have to watch what publishers, bookstores, the Internet and search engines are doing. For people who are very busy, it might also be a good idea to focus only on critical success factors (Abels, 2002).

From the work of other authors (e.g. Costa, 1995; Holmes, McElwee and Thomas, 1995; Pashiardis, 1996; Slaughter,

1999; Voros, 2001) we can also gather that environmental scanning should help us to come up with suggestions for improvement in a particular direction and that we can use both formal and informal sources. Environmental scanning is about using all information resources that may give you a competitive advantage. It therefore takes a much wider perspective of the environment in which people/organisations are operating in order to cover a much wider spectrum. It is not just about noting information, but about noting the information that needs to be put to use in order to *survive*, and not merely keeping a research edge. For example, a company can have a group of researchers who are using the latest equipment to explore new solutions to security systems. If their marketing efforts and their understanding of their clientele are not keeping up, or if they do not note what their competition is doing, they may still not be successful. The same would apply to LIS professionals who note the latest trends, such as the commercialisation of search engines (which was prominent at the time of writing this book), but without also considering, for example, increased Internet access because of cheaper access due to competition between service providers, or governments announcing free access to certain states or regions, and the effect this may have on their users.

In the context of environmental scanning, consider the following quotation from Zhuge Liang (c. 200 AD, *The Way of the General*):

There are three avenues of opportunity: events, trends, and conditions. When opportunities occur through events but you are unable to respond, you are not smart. When opportunities become active through a trend and yet you cannot make plans, you are not wise. When opportunities emerge through conditions, but you cannot act on them, you are not bold. Those skilled in generalship always achieve their victories by taking advantage of opportunities. (Choo, 2002)

Opportunities are exactly what we hope to note through our use of alerting services. If we hope to use these in securing our professional positions, it is therefore necessary to learn from environmental scanning to broaden our concept of alerting services. We should take a wider perspective and differentiate 'information' from 'noting information', and from 'survival' and 'required for survival'.

The link between alerting services and retrospective searching

The terms 'current awareness services', 'alerting services' and 'SDI' were initially used to distinguish them from retrospective searches. It was recognised that LIS users can have different types of needs; for example, they might need a factual piece of information, such as the name of the capital city of France, or the average income in the UK. Sometimes, however, users need to find as much information as possible on a topic, for example, when starting a research project, preparing for a conference paper or working on a dissertation or thesis. A search strategy is formulated for the topic. For instance, when using the Dialog command language to find data on the information needs of oncology nurses from a Dialog database such as Medline or Cancerlit, this would be: 'information(2n)need? AND oncology(w)nurs?' If the search strategy is run against a database to find all information in the database, or the information published during a specific period, such as the last five years or the last year, it is referred to as a retrospective search, in other words, searching backwards in time. In the early days of electronic access to information, retrospective searches were mostly run against databases, such as the databases available through Dialog. Retrospective searching can, however, also mean searching the library catalogue for books on a topic, or working through printed indexes, browsing the shelves, and so on. It is often a one-off search for information, to establish what has been published on a particular topic. This does not mean that the search strategy cannot be adapted, or completely changed during the whole process of seeking information. The essence of retrospective searching is to establish what has been published in the past up till the most recent publications, or during a specific period of time. Sometimes such search strategies were also saved as search profiles for alerting services.

As explained in preceding sections, CAS and alerting services concern current information, that is, information made available for the first time. Although retrospective searches and CAS each serve a different purpose, they can be used to supplement each other. A retrospective search for research for a doctoral thesis can be continued through alerting services to ensure that a researcher keeps track with developments during the research period. Using alerting services can, however, also lead to the need for retrospective searches. It can, for example be noted that there is increased interest in providing information services suitable for disabled users. To get a clearer picture of the needs of disabled users, one or more retrospective searches might be necessary. When redefining alerting services, the link with retrospective searches and putting information to use should be explicitly pointed out: the use of alerting services should not be seen as an isolated action.

Why are we offering alerting services?

Before redefining alerting services, we will consider the reasons for offering such services. It seems appropriate to move from the traditional understanding to a reflection on what our rationale should be in today's society. I will therefore start with the traditional reasons for offering CAS as explained in the early literature.

When LIS started to offer CAS it was promoted as a means to take note of the latest information and developments. From the early works of Hamilton (1995), Kemp (1979) and Whitehall (1982) it appears that CAS were mostly offered to keep users informed on matters that were considered important to a profession, such as upcoming events, the activities of colleagues or attitudes and developments. The intention was to make people aware of the existence of information that might come in handy at some time in the future. It was furthermore argued that CAS could save users time in searching for information – because the CAS were offered to users by LIS professionals.

Based on an analysis of the works on traditional CAS as well as electronic and Web CAS, Fourie (1999a) reconsidered the benefits (and therefore also the reasons) of Web CAS:

- keeping track of new developments in a particular field(s) of interest;

- keeping track of new websites, discussion groups (listservs, Usenet groups), publications;

- keeping track of trends in a particular field of interest (e.g. by means of the tables of contents of journals);

- keeping track of Internet-related developments (e.g. search engines);

- taking note of daily events of interest (e.g. as reported in newspapers);

- taking note of developments by competing markets (e.g. changes to a company's website);

- having intelligent agents learn from your preferences and filtering information accordingly;

- receiving customised information on, for example, the weather report;

- keeping track of new documents added to a database of which it took note (e.g. records in a database such as ERIC or new sites indexed by a search engine).

These reasons point to an intention to make people aware of a variety of information coming from a variety of resources. They also point to the use of intelligent software to learn from our preferences for information. There is, however, still no mentioning of moving on to actions and taking up opportunities.

Redefining alerting services and our reasons for using them

If we wish to use alerting services to seize opportunities we should have a clear idea of what we understand by 'seizing' and 'opportunities'. Opportunity can be interpreted as a favourable situation, or good chance. Seizing means trying to grasp, clutch at, snatch greedily, hold firmly, tackle differently, greedy of gain, getting hold of and comprehend. Seizing opportunities can therefore be interpreted as firm actions towards a definitive goal – namely a favourable situation or desirable chance. Environmental scanning especially is aimed at enabling organisations to secure and improve their positions. To make the best use of alerting services, it might therefore be time to reconsider our interpretation of the concept and perhaps also borrow from other methods, such as environmental scanning, that might help us to widen our interpretation to ensure that we gain from our efforts. It might further be necessary to widen the scope of what we are monitoring as well as our intention with monitoring. From the literature on forecasting we should, however, also be sensitive to the unpredictability of our environment and the difficulty of 'forecasting' where and how we should position ourselves (Slaughter, 1999; Karim, 2004).

To use alerting services to seize opportunities effectively, we require a change of mind-set. For example, if I use alerting services to put myself in a favourable position, what do I hope to gain from it? First, I will need to reflect on my idea of favourable opportunities, what I am looking for, and so on. This will be very personal, and difficult to determine. It takes us back to the uncertainties of information needs, the anxiety to bridge a gap between where we are and what we know, and where we need or want to be. It takes us back to Dervin's (1999) link between information needs and sense making. We need to make sense of our individual situations, needs, desires, and factors that will influence us in being successful. Such factors can, for example, be our own personalities and learning styles. We need to make sense of what we need to monitor, and we need to make sense of what we are monitoring. (These aspects will be dealt with in more detail in a later chapter.) Making sense of our situation and environment and the information that might help us in positioning ourselves favourably in our jobs, will be more difficult than when searching for factual information or retrospective searches, but certainly not impossible. Such sense-making will require practice, reflection, and unfortunately also a lot of self-doubt. As Wilson (1993) explains: 'But, apart from this, the only kind of currency that may seem worthwhile is currency over areas of immediate practical relevance to the individual ... People manage to live in what are, in effect, microscopic worlds, excluding and ignoring practically all of the world around them'. Deciding what we hope to achieve on an individual level will be difficult, and may greatly differ.

Based on the preceding discussions of the traditional views of CAS and alerting services, as well as environmental scanning, I do have some general expectations from alerting services. Before explaining these, I would like to set the reader's mind at rest: I do not think that our professional lives are just about going out, walking over people and taking what we think we deserve! Life is not just about opportunities, but there is also no need to miss out on something because we were not smart, wise or bold enough. Even if we keep a balance between 'personal life' and 'work', we can and should look for opportunities and professional fulfilment in our jobs.

Although I will take a wider look at alerting services than the traditional view, the reader should interpret this as a 'generalised' view. It should be tailored and scaled down by individuals according to their specific needs and situations, as no individual can be expected to use alerting services on such a comprehensive scale. (More guidance on deciding on the objectives with using alerting services and selecting appropriate services will be given in a later chapter.) The use of alerting services should be aimed at the benefit of the organisation/institution for which you are working, but especially also at the development of your full potential.

What would I expect from the use of alerting services?

Personally, I would hope that the use of alerting services would help me with the following:

- *Taking note of potentially useful information*: I would like to be aware of new (potentially useful) information that becomes available (i.e. information that is disseminated for the first time) that might help me in achieving my goal. I therefore first need to be able to clearly formulate my goal in terms of opportunities, and what I hope to achieve. Sometimes information might have been around for some time, and I might not have picked up on it. My alert support system (e.g. a colleague or discussion list) should then help me to note such information. Retrospective searches that may fill up the gaps might also be useful. It is important to note that the usefulness of information will depend on what we hope to achieve by noting information. As our reasons are different from early CAS/alerting services, it also means that the types of information that will be potentially useful will be very different. It is no longer just about keeping a research edge. (The variety of information also comes through in the following point.) Furthermore, there will be very different and individual interpretations of what potentially useful information entails.

- *Taking note of a variety of types of information*: I would like to be able to scan a variety of types of information that might be potentially useful, such as factual information, opinion papers, research reports, dissertations, advertisements, calls for papers, calls for people to get involved, useful websites, product announcements, and so on – whatever information might be useful for the particular situation in which I find myself at a particular point in time. (Although it is not my personal favourite, even office gossip might well be useful – unfortunately people sometimes tend to rely only on the latter. This is also referred to as minding the professional grapevine.) It is no longer just scientific information and research findings or what the competitors are doing that need to be monitored.

- *Monitoring a variety of formats of information*: I would like to be able to scan a variety of formats in which information might become available, such as print, electronic or oral. I would like to scan formal as well as informal, external as well as internal resources for disseminating information.

- *Monitoring a variety of information resources in an attempt to identify potentially useful information*: I would like to be able to make a choice between a variety of information resources that I monitor and services that I can use. My choice will depend on what I need at a particular point in time, what I can afford, the ease of use, and so on. I would like to reconsider my information needs and adapt my choice of information resources and services at any point in time as I see fit.

- *Knowing that the information is as current as possible*: I would like to know about the information as soon as it is disseminated for the first time. Timing is very, very important.

- *Scope*: I would like to scan any variety and combination of topics that I consider necessary.

- *Purpose*: I would like to be able to achieve a variety of purposes, such as noting trends, new developments, job opportunities, new skills required, meeting with the demands from society, avoiding surprises, etc.

I would *love* it if intelligent software could monitor my use of information resources, link it to my personality and learning style profiles as well as skills and recommend actions. As this is still way in the future, I will have to make other efforts to ensure that the results of using alerting services are not merely noting information, but may turn to action. I would therefore like to build in some mechanism that will remind me to reflect on the information and think: what opportunities might there be in this?

This is all still close to the traditional reasons for using CAS or alerting services, as well as the reasons for using Web CAS. There is, however, a stronger emphasis on the variety of information, the need to monitor whatever might be necessary and the use of information. We especially need to work on bridging the gap between noting information, becoming alert to the implications and taking appropriate actions.

Reinterpreting alerting services

In this book, the pragmatic interpretation of alerting services will be the use of any service or method that can help an individual such as myself or a group of people to note information that they may find useful (with regard to furthering their careers) when first disseminated, regardless of the information, the format of the information or the method of information dissemination.

In a more academic sense, this book will use alerting services to describe a collection of services and methods selected and employed according to the specific needs and specifications of a user (e.g. an individual, a group, or a larger body such as a professional organisation, a company or a business) in order to become aware of what is currently happening in the professional, organisational and societal environment that may have an impact on them. Such services should also make the user aware of what is currently happening in a particular field of interest, problem area, task, and so on. The spectrum of services should enable the user to cover trends, factual information, research results, opportunities, patterns and so on, according to specific needs and expectations of the value of current awareness and being alert. The services can be used in a variety of media and formats (formal as well as informal). The information can be in the form of article titles and abstracts (e.g. as in a table of contents), newspaper clippings, conference calls for papers indicating the themes currently of interest, announcements of new book titles, or notices of professional workshops. It can be in printed form, electronic records from a database, or websites with information. (The different methods and media will be explained in more detail in Chapter 4.) The services and methods that we select will be influenced by availability, affordability, specific perceptions of what is needed and the benefits that can be gained. To be of real value, however, information that the user becomes aware of (current awareness) needs to be evaluated for further usefulness and stored and organised in a personal system (e.g. an electronic database, personal filing system, website or weblog). Although mechanisms for recording noted information and exploiting these in making decisions are not traditionally part of our definitions of current awareness/ alerting services, inclusion might more explicitly strengthen the need to find ways of using alerting services to gain a competitive edge. Once again, we can note the warning by Nicholas and Dobrowolski (1999: 232) 'looking for personal inspiration will become more important than looking for what is now called information'. Awareness of current information as perceived in the traditional CAS and alerting services is no longer enough: in fact awareness should be followed by action or at least the willingness and readiness to react if we really wish to benefit from the use of alerting services.

'Alert' means paying full attention to what is happening, being fully aware of something, being ready to deal with anything that may happen and watching out. According to the Merriam-Webster Online Dictionary, alert also means 'watchful and prompt to meet danger or emergency; quick to perceive and act'. It means that you are aware of dangers, and that you are prepared to react. This can certainly also be interpreted to allow for opportunities.

If we move from 'awareness' to 'alertness' it will require more time, effort and energy to deal with information, and certainly more uncertainty on whether we are taking the right actions and whether we are monitoring the right things. Reflection on the actions we need to take will take even more time. However, the counterquestion to ask is whether we can afford not to be alert in the context, as explained in this chapter?

When expanding our interpretation of alerting services, it is also necessary to explicitly acknowledge the link between the use of alerting services and retrospective searching. Useful information picked up through alerting services should be supplemented with retrospective searches before making decisions.

Conclusion

In the preceding section, I have argued for expanding our interpretation of alerting services, and widening the scope of information that we are monitoring. Our reasons for using alerting services will be very individual and should be linked to what we hope to gain by using these services: seizing opportunities and surviving. In this context, it was also pointed out that the use of alerting services should not be seen in isolation: it should be linked to the use of retrospective searches, and our knowledge of information needs and information seeking behaviour. The latter will feature more strongly in the following chapters.

If we accept that LIS professionals are facing a very challenging environment requiring drastic measures for professional survival, and that alerting services should do more than simply make us aware of the existence of new information, the next step would be to reflect on the dynamic professional environment in which we find ourselves and what implications timely actions may have for LIS professionals. We often think that we are keeping track and doing our bit, but is this in fact so, and is this enough? How can we do more – but without being overwhelmed and driven to despair by too much information?

3

A dynamic LIS environment and the need to be a benchmark

Introduction

LIS professionals find themselves in a dynamic, exiting and very harsh global environment. They find themselves in a situation where they need to fight for professional survival and recognition. 'Disintermediation reaches the living room', 'jumping off the disintermediation bandwagon' and 'future proofing the profession' are just some of the expressions that have been heard. More recently, with regard to developments concerning Google and new jobs for information professionals, Steve Arnold declared, 'You are the last bastion, you know how to deal with things like provenance ... you know how to assess whether the query is accurate' (cited by Hyams, 2005: 1).

Although we have always been aware of the importance of keeping up with developments, the pressure has increased. We have to compete with fellow professionals, as well as professionals from other fields claiming new roles on our terrain. We have to deal with all kinds of pressures. Quality control, performance appraisal, best practices, lifelong learning, continuing professional development, benchmarking, competitiveness, creativity, innovation, and dynamic and proactive reaction are some of the words driving the twenty-first century LIS professional. These words can drive people to despair, over the edge – or to new heights and exciting opportunities. It all depends on how you mentally prepare yourself for these challenges, where you find information to guide your decisions, and what you know and understand about your specific situation and the driving forces. It requires people to take note of what is happening, and also to *do* something about it. As explained in the previous chapter, it requires people to be alert.

There are many opportunities for those who are alert. In the context of intermediary searching, Barbara Quint (2005), for example, declares, 'Perhaps it's time for us professional searchers to pick up our lanterns and go looking for our lost sheep. Now we have to be careful. If we make too much noise or start waving our hands about, they may take fright and scatter.' She continues: 'Now that online information has moved so many of the tasks formerly performed as intermediated searches to end users, we professional searchers have the time to pursue new opportunities for service. Once again, the cry goes forth, 'What's next?' and the answer is another question – 'Who's next?'

One can proclaim the end of libraries and information services, or like Barbara Quint, one can embrace the thrill of preparing for new opportunities. To be honest, it is not always such a thrill: I often find myself very uncertain of what I am doing, whether it is worthwhile, and whether I have made the best decisions. On the other hand, if I do not believe that it is thrilling (at least most of the time), it might be very tempting to just give up, and to merely note the basics to get my job done ... and to join the chorus of complaints about other people taking all the opportunities. It is all too easy to declare that there are so many things happening that it is useless to even try and keep up with everything!

This book is not about trying to keep up with all things new. It is about taking an informed decision about how much there is out there that might be worth monitoring, and how much you would be able to handle. Evidently, you can't monitor everything, but you can at least make a small effort – but make it an effort that will matter to you and your career. It is also about taking an informed guess about what to monitor, to watch how you benefit from it, and to reconsider your choices if they do not work out. There is no perfect recipe for what we need to monitor, and there will never be.

One condolence is, that (the right) efforts to keep up with developments, might have a snowball effect – your efforts might lead to other opportunities, for example, experts being asked to review books and conference papers, and so on – all contributing to being alert. According to Wilson (1993) 'The only ones who can maintain a high degree of currency over a field are those who have already invested heavily in acquisition of that field's stock of knowledge and in developing the relevant interpretative ability'. Although it takes time and effort to get to such a point in one's professional life, it is something worth striving for. Many LIS professionals can serve as examples. Names that come to mind are Reva Basch (*http: //www.jereva.com/reva.html*), Phil Bradley (*http: //www.philb.com/*), Mary Ellen Bates (*http: //www.batesinfo.com/*) and Greg Notess (*http: //www.notess.com/*), and many other practitioners. There are also many academics that set the tone such as Tom Wilson (*http: //www.shef.ac.uk/is/wilson/*), Marcia Bates (*http: //www.gseis.ucla.edu/faculty/bates/*), and Peter Ingwersen (*http: //www.db.dk/pi/*). If you check out their websites you will see that they are all very active, but also very human: they have hobbies and they have loved-ones.

Amidst concerns about the survival of the LIS profession, discouragement with new roles being grabbed by other fields and professions, and disgust about how professionals from other fields are offering typical library functions, it seems timely to take a positive look at how LIS professionals can use their expertise in alerting services to survive, and to seize new opportunities coming their way. To do so, we first need to understand our situation in our professional environment. We also need to understand that we as individuals are central in this environment, and that our perceptions of the environment and its requirements, as well as our perceptions of ourselves and the power of information in decision making and creativity will influence our use of alerting services and the action we will take. Our situation will also influence our reluctance to react. In fact, our situation also includes our feelings (affective experiences such as anxiety, frustrations and excitement), knowledge and understanding (cognitive abilities).

From the start, one should realise that it is not possible to keep track of everything taking place in the world around. One should prioritise. While growing into a culture of alertness as explained in the previous chapter, one should initially limit one's focus, rather than trying to be too ambitious. Alerting services should be like a daily injection of energy and inspiration. They should not be a burden. Based on an analysis of your own situation, especially including an analysis of yourself, you should demarcate the environment you intend to monitor.

A first step would be to understand and plot the scope of the environment. In this regard it is important to note that we need to consider the following:

- what the environment is expecting of us (as individual LIS professionals and as a profession);

- what we are expecting from ourselves with regard to the changing environment (as individuals and as a profession).

In order to decide which part of the environment to monitor, LIS professionals need to understand their work environment and their role and position in this environment: what are their tasks and responsibilities, and how can they exploit alerting services? They should also bear in mind their personal interest, individual preferences and where and how they would like to make a difference. Know your immediate environment and know yourself! In addition, ask yourself how 'greedy' you are to seize opportunities! Furthermore, bear in mind that determining what you need to know is certainly a very difficult task, as we have learned from theories of information seeking behaviour and from our experiences in reference work. Your information needs will also depend on your levels of anxiety: how critical is it for you to note new information?

One way of getting a clearer picture of oneself in the larger environment is to do a brainstorming session with colleagues or to draw mind maps. Lateral and creative thinking will especially be important. It is also possible to plot oneself in the different environments that need monitoring.

The purpose of this chapter is to take a more pragmatic view of how LIS professionals can consider their environment and make choices for where and how they will focus their awareness of developments. A few influences that might be worth monitoring will be discussed. These are not nearly exhaustive and should be adapted according to individual circumstances. Start small by focusing on fewer things, and leaving enough time to use these to make a difference. As we learn more and as our understanding of our environment and the impact of developments deepen, it will become easier to take on more.

But let's first consider what is important to use in our professional environment.

What is important to us?

Depending on the environment in which we are working, there may be more or less pressure to note current information and changes in the environment.

The expectations from our immediate jobs are linked to the goals and visions of the immediate wider environment in which the job needs to be completed, such as the academic library, and the institution, such as a university or college. All institutions form part of a larger society. First there is the local society, such as a particular city, province or county, next the national society, such as a particular country, and then the international, global society. Lots of things are happening here that we should note. It is easy to argue that it is impossible to note everything, but we should at least understand enough about the environment in which we are working to identify the most noteworthy aspects and take an informed decision on what we need to monitor.

In demarcating the environment to be monitored, the following can be considered:

- What is important for your particular situation?

- How can you expect to benefit from alerting services?

- How do you look at the environment?

- Who is your competition and what are they doing?

- What are monitored by professional organisations?

- How can you collaborate with others?

The following sections will address these questions in more detail.

Determining what is important

Before deciding on which parts of the environment to focus, LIS professionals should consider their professional situation and needs. The following list of questions might be a useful point of departure. It is, however, not intended as an exhaustive list. The questions should be adapted according to specific circumstances:

- *What is absolutely essential to note for your job?* For example, new labour laws, salary increases, serious fluctuations in foreign currencies and exchange rates.

- *What might have an impact on your job and the services you are planning?* For example, new school curricula, or government support to increase information literacy levels and access to technology.

- *What might be worth monitoring so that you can react in time?* For example, noting new trends in IT developments, or trends in other countries. Examples of the latter include the emphasis on social inclusion, catering for the needs of disabled people, advocacy for open access, making public libraries attractive to the younger generation, working with refugees and asylum seekers, personal privacy in the digital environment and catering for the needs of older people searching the Internet. The international concern with increased plagiarism due to easy access to electronic information is certainly also worth noting.

- *What is the focus of your job?* For example, indexing, classification, management, information literacy skills. It goes without saying that you should note such changes.

- *Which skills are required in the changing environment?* For example, skills in time and stress management, interpersonal or communication skills.

- *What might impress other people?* For example, throwing around the latest buzzwords or industry product names or expertly citing the latest statistics. (Being alert is, however, not about impressing people, but about making a difference.)

- *What will really give you a competitive edge against colleagues or other organisations?* What will help you to ensure that you are better than them, and that you are prepared for changes in the environment, when they actually come about?

- *What do you need to note?* For example, developments, the opinions of others or new products.

- *Which events should you note?* At which conferences and workshops can you learn new skills, and where should you be seen?

- *What would you enjoy doing and what would fit in with your personality?* For example, teaching, planning, advocacy, organising.

Benefiting from alerting services

Before plotting the sections of the environment where you wish to focus, you also need to reflect on the value of the information you will be collecting. The following are suggestions of a few questions you might like to ask:

- How will you benefit by noting this information? How will you benefit by reflecting on the information? What motivation/rewards are there for you in being alert?

- Will the information help you to take a decision? What decisions have you taken in the past based on similar information?

- Are you working in an organisational climate where new initiatives are encouraged (i.e. can you expect to receive recognition and encouragement for initiatives)?

- What kind of focus will bring career rewards as well as career fulfilment and job satisfaction (i.e. what will bring you joy)?

Different ways of looking at the professional environment

An OCLC environmental scanning report notes the following:

> ...[W]hat we conceive about our business is not sufficient to fully understand all the effects that are actually happening in and around our business... [W]e are completely unable to perceive of all the dynamics of our business environment because our conception limits our perception. Our accumulation of, and intense focus on, our knowledge controls what we believe. And, what we believe controls what we are able to see. What haven't you noticed lately? (OCLC, 2003: vii)

When monitoring developments it is therefore not just about what you notice, but also about what you do not notice. Even if you are presented with information, it does not automatically follow that you will also note the implications or trends and developments that may follow from this. The latter is a skill that needs to be cultured and developed.

From information seeking studies we have learned that information seeking is often aimed at making sense of situations (Dervin, 1999). We experience a gap or discrepancy between what we know and what we need to know. When thinking about what we need to know to plan for the future, it is even more difficult to decide what 'gaps' we need to try and bridge. We may experience different levels of anxiety depending on how important we consider the information to be, and how important it is to us to bridge the gap (Wilson et al., 2002). Our anxiety may also be more acute if we doubt our abilities to deal with the information we may find.

Information seeking studies also showed the following:

- Our tasks and the environment in which we work will have a very strong impact on our information seeking behaviour, and therefore certainly also on our use of alerting services. Vakkari (2003) gives an excellent review of research on task-based information searching. Different jobs and tasks will have different requirements and demands for the latest information.

- We are all individuals with very diverse skills, personalities, abilities, preferences etc. that will influence our information seeking behaviour. These will also influence the choices we make in what we would like to focus on in using alerting services, and how we put information to use. This is a very simplified explanation; one should not underestimate the complexities of these issues. Although many of these issues have already been addressed in the research literature, there is still tremendous scope for research linked to alerting services.

- Although the environment in which we find ourselves is very complex and demanding, we only deal with a small section of it. This will influence the information we will monitor. However, it is still necessary to recognise how vast this environment really is, and to admit that by using alerting services we are choosing to scale down what we are monitoring. From the literature on environmental scanning, the previous chapter has shown that we need to scan both internal and external resources. When we scale down, we should explicitly acknowledge our decisions and our rationale for them.

- Our information needs are dynamic and will change over time; our needs change as we learn more and as our understanding increases.

- Tasks have different levels of complexities and requirements for information. This is clear, for example, from the research by Byström (2002). Although there is no consensus about how to define a 'task' (Vakkari, 2003) we can accept that it has an impact on information seeking behaviour. Along with other factors, it should also influence how we demarcate the environment we wish to monitor.

- We should not underestimate the impact of learning style and personality on information seeking behaviour, as these will also impact on choices in the use of alerting services and what we intend to monitor. These will be explored in more detail in Chapter 5.

In writing this chapter, I considered many ways of how one can look at the professional environment. The following are some of the ideas that came up for points of departure that we can use to demarcate the section of the 'environment' we intend to monitor. I am not using the phrase 'wish to monitor' here, as what we may wish to do and the realities of what time, energy and other resources allow for might be very different things. Although the most logical way of demarcating the environment into sections to be monitored would be a systems approach (which I will discuss), I believe it is also necessary to allow for other more personal approaches. If we want to use alerting services successfully, it is important to recognise that we are central to the environment, and that many of our choices will depend on our personal interpretations and what works for us.

Considering our tasks and the environment

As has been explained, there is a very close relationship between information seeking behaviour and professional tasks and workplace environments. We all have our specific jobs: we may be working in an academic library, public library or medical library. We may be working for vendors or aggregator services such as Dialog or Ebsco Host. We may be lecturers, researchers or information brokers. Each environment and each task will bring its own responsibilities for keeping up, as well as its own expectations. We can either take a very specific look at our job, or we can take a more holistic view in trying to see the larger picture. This 'view' will probably also be influenced by whether we are just expected to get a job done, or whether we are expected to lead the way.

- *Micro-worlds (very specific)*: We can take immediate tasks and responsibilities as our 'environment', for example, what is happening with regard to book indexing, metadata or reference work. If we take this approach, it should not be too difficult to demarcate what we need to monitor. A book indexer would, for example, monitor advertisements of and reports on indexing software, publications on freelance indexing, new reference works available for free via the Web, textbooks or subject-specific guides on book indexing, announcements of conferences and workshops and announcements of indexing awards. For those who do not have a lot of work experience or experience in the use of alerting services, it might be a good idea to first focus on the micro-world – that is, information that might be of immediate use. Even when taking a micro-world view, you may be overwhelmed with information. It also seems as if somebody who needs to focus on getting a job done would benefit more from a micro-view than attempting too much.

- *Meso-worlds*: We can take our immediate tasks and responsibilities within a particular organisation or profession as point of departure. We will monitor the same kind of things as for the micro-world, but we will also need to monitor what is happening in the larger context, such as the organisation (e.g. new regulations, new policies, new visions), or perhaps the profession (e.g. initiatives taken by different indexing societies, or interests in web indexing). In a meso-world view, there is slightly more emphasis on seeing the larger picture, which will mean monitoring more information and requiring more insight to interpret information.

- *Macro-world*: In addition to our immediate tasks and responsibilities, and our organisation, we can also look at what is happening in the country, what is happening internationally and what is happening in the profession that might have an influence on our information needs. People interested in noting holistic trends may take this view of the environment. In the case of indexers, I would, for example, think that the chairperson of the indexing society or other leading figure would consider developments in the publishing or database industry and how this may affect the role of indexers. Taking a 'macro-world' view will mean a diverse information resources needs to be monitored. I would recommend this only to people who really need to monitor trends and set the tone. Collaboration in this regard might be a good idea. Taking the example of indexers, different board members of an indexing society might, for example, decide to monitor different facets of the 'macro' environment.

Considering uncertainty and the urgency for new information

From decades of information seeking studies we have learned that information needs are often based on uncertainty and anxiety. Although this applies to all information seeking and also information monitoring, there may be circumstances where it is more pressing and acute, for example, if you are heading a library or information service that is fighting for survival and need to convince both management and users of the usefulness of your service. You might then be under more pressure to monitor a wider spectrum of the environment than would otherwise be the case.

Harris (as cited by Wilson et al., 2002) notes that uncertainty has a long history of association with decision-making research: 'Decision-making is the process of sufficiently reducing uncertainty and doubt about alternatives to allow a reasonable choice to be made from among them'. In deciding which actions we need to take to survive as LIS professionals, we need to make sense of our environment and what is happening. Decision makers will probably experience anxiety more intensely than people who are merely expected to work according to orders (e.g. issuing books at the reference desk). The same would apply to LIS services feeling really threatened.

Taking anxiety and uncertainty as point of departure, I would like to distinguish the following approaches to demarcating the environment to be monitored by using alerting services.

- *Let somebody else worry,* or *hope the boss knows what is happening*: Although it is nice to note new information, you do not really consider it to be your responsibility. Your levels of anxiety and uncertainty are very low.

- *Setting an example to the junior staff*: Your main anxiety is to be able to set an example to other staff members. Noting *some* new information/developments would therefore be sufficient. It is not necessary to note as much as is possible.

- *Where do I take the LIS service?* As a LIS manager/ director there might be more pressure on you to monitor a wider spectrum of the environment, such as in the macro-world. I would imagine that column writers, journal editors, and freelance consultants would probably find themselves in a similar position. For the latter, it might even be a case of survival.

- *How will we survive?* If it is your responsibility to prove the value of a LIS service or to maintain your position as a benchmark to other LIS services, one can expect levels of anxiety to be very high.

Considering ambition

Although the use of alerting services in this book has to do with professional responsibility, it is also pretty much about ambition – seizing new opportunities. Ambition is basically about what's in it for me? The more ambitious one is, the stronger the reasons for using alerting services. Highly ambitious people would probably be more likely to see the value in spending time and effort on being alert. If one takes ambition as point of departure to demarcate the environment, the following can apply:

- *Happy with who I am, no need to change*: There is probably very little interest in the use of alerting services – at most the need to monitor announcements of training opportunities or conferences.

- *It might be nice to follow a few trends that suit my interest*: Using alerting services might be nice, but need not be taken too seriously.

- *Need to keep up my benchmarks and standards*: Using alerting services becomes serious and it would probably be necessary to scan a wider spectrum of the environment, such as in a meso or macro-world view.

- *I need to impress and set the trend*: Once again, the use of alerting services is serious and would depend on scanning a wider spectrum of the environment, such as in a meso or macro-world view.

Philantrophic approach

There are still many LIS professionals that feel very strongly about the role of libraries, for example, concerning free access to information, social inclusion, literacy and information literacy and bridging the digital divide. If this is the case, it would be essential to take a macro-world view in scanning as much as possible of the environment (e.g. monitoring new laws and regulation, initiatives by other role players, and so on), to see where you might make a difference.

Systems approach

In the systems approach, I would like to describe the task environment of LIS professionals as consisting of different layers, starting with a very specific layer of the immediate task that needs to be completed. LIS professionals can find themselves in a specific section offering information literacy programmes in an academic library, the reference section in a public library or the acquisitions section in a special library. (This can be related to the micro-world view.) Each section comes with specific tasks, expectations for completing these, expectations for showing professional growth, and expectations for innovative contributions and the need to add value to the wider organisation. We have a job to do, and to a greater or lesser extent it may be required of us to keep up in this job. Taking this approach, individuals will need to figure out for themselves, which layers of the environment they wish to monitor, and in how much depth. In the use of alerting services, depth as well as breadth is very important.

In trying to be alert to developments in the environment, LIS professionals should realise the following:

1. There are different layers in this environment, for example, the:
    — immediate working environment, namely the specific job they are doing (e.g. cataloguing or reference work);
    — organisation in which they are working (e.g. library in an academic institution);
    — country (national) environment; and
    — global (international) environment.

    The different layers consist of different sections or sectors. We can also think of these as landscapes. In the wider environment – national as well as international – these landscapes include the professional, economic, political and technological (IT) landscapes, as well as many others.

2. Our perceptions of the changes and pressures we note, as well as our perceptions of how important these are to our specific situation, will influence our decisions on what we will monitor from the environment, how much time we will spend on this, and so on. This will influence our need for alerting services.

3. LIS professionals are standing in this environment with their colleagues, peers and competitors. If they want to make the best of the information, they also need to understand themselves as individuals, to know their preferences, learning styles, strengths, weakness, and so on. Being alert is not just about noting information, but putting information to use. It is about securing our positions and putting ourselves in better positions. Where and how would we like to make a difference with the information we have noted? What will give us career rewards as well as personal satisfaction?

What are others doing?

The previous chapter explained that the use of alerting services as seen in this book is different from the traditional view of CAS or alerting services: it is not just about noting new information. If we want to position ourselves well, it will therefore also be necessary to monitor what other people in our environment are doing – especially our competition.

Peers, competitors and people from other professions

We can argue that we do not have time for alerting services and everything that goes with them. However, our arguments seem less convincing when we are surrounded with people who do seem to have the time to stay abreast and to make a difference. Nesbeitt and Gordon (2002: 51), for example, state that many LIS professionals read the professional literature, and discuss new developments that may have an impact. They also stress that although we might think that we do not have the time for alerting services, we also cannot afford not to make the time.

There are many people in the LIS profession who can serve as role models for how to stay abreast. I have already mentioned some names in the beginning of this chapter. Practising LIS professionals should especially search for other practitioners as role models. It might be an interesting exercise to identify such role models by using questionnaires through professional associations. Instead of 'who is the most beautiful woman in the world?', or 'who made the biggest impact in the twentieth century?', we could have: 'who is the most alert LIS professional?' In-depth interviews with such role models might shed light on how they monitor information – and put it to use, because the latter is what distinguishes them from the rest. It might also be worthwhile to do a content analysis of their personal websites to see how they are actually putting information to use – and how they share it with others. A further aspect we might consider is whether such role models cooperate and learn form each other, and to what extent. In the OCLC (2003: 69) report on environmental scanning, it is noted that, 'Sustainability is only possible through collaboration'. One wonders if the same would apply when seizing opportunities in the LIS world.

Apart from noting how LIS professionals are using alerting services, one should also note how people from other professions are alerted to changes in their environment. It should be especially worthwhile to consider people from competitive professions such as IT professionals and booksellers. Perhaps we feel there is nothing we can learn from other professions. It has, however, often been stated that other professions are seizing opportunities from the LIS field. They are a threat to LIS professionals as they often take the opportunities LIS professionals believe they are entitled to, and should therefore be considered as very real competition. Our question should be: how do they manage to do so?

Professional associations and bodies

In a certain sense, LIS professionals are on their own when it comes to noting events that will affect them in particular. They are, however, also part of the larger LIS profession where changes affect the profession as a whole, which in turn means that such changes and developments should be noted by the profession as a whole. One way of keeping up with developments would therefore be to become a member of a professional association such as the Charted Institute of Library and Information Professionals (CILIP) or the American Library Association (ALA); indeed, there are many more such professional associations. According to Palmer (2004) professional organisations such as CILIP should get involved in 'horizon scanning' – to see the bigger picture in terms of trends and developments and to alert professionals to these. Not all professional associations, however, are equally active in noting and setting trends. A first step would be to identify the 'environment' monitored by the professional body, and how active it is in this process. The next chapter will offer more detail on using professional associations as alerting services.

Sharing responsibility

LIS professionals also belong to a larger profession, and can work with fellow professionals in monitoring the environment, and in taking proactive decisions in dealing with this environment. They are not alone. They do not need to attempt to cope with everything on their own. As we will see from trends noted for the LIS environment, as well as society in general, there is a strong movement to collaborative work, collaborative learning and collaborative information seeking. This means that collaboration is certainly something LIS professionals should exploit in their efforts to seize new opportunities. How can they work together to manage the vastness of environmental developments?

Groups of people with similar interests may also work together, for example, people working for the same LIS or academic department. Although a growing interest in collaborative work and collaborative information seeking is reported, we still have a very long way to go in order to sort out issues of trust, competition, and so on.

Lastly we should consider the possibility of collaborating with colleagues in spreading the 'burden' of using alerting services. A wider spectrum of the environment might be covered by dividing the different landscapes or sectors between participants. Although this will certainly be a very useful approach, there will be much to consider, such as equal spread of the workload, trust, reliability, competition between peers and colleagues, and so on.

More suggestions on cooperating in the use of alerting services will be given in a later chapter.

Different sectors of the environment

The OCLC (2003) report on environmental scanning noted a number of things of which a few will be mentioned here as indicators of what might be important in positioning ourselves. (More information can be found at *http: // www.oclc.org/reports/2003escan.htm.*) The report refers to subsections of the environment as landscapes. It distinguishes between social, economic, technology, research and learning landscapes, as well as library landscapes. A few of their observations for each will be noted here in order to indicate the value of monitoring different sections of the environment.

Social landscape

There seems a very strong emphasis on consumer characteristics such as satisfaction, seamlessness and self-service. The report therefore argues that libraries should consider this in planning their services, for example, by designing simpler interfaces looking more like Google and accepting users' styles of information seeking. 'Instead of wringing our hands over students using the Web for research, we should help them learn to use Web materials and resources more effectively' (OCLC, 2003: 9). The roles of interactivity and gaming in the lives of young people are also mentioned. If taken seriously this can lead to many new initiatives and research opportunities for LIS professionals, for example, in providing a seamless customer experience and trying to enter users' spaces instead of making them come to our spaces, to name but a few.

Economic landscape

In the economic landscape there seems to be a worldwide trend towards slow economic growth that will affect funding for education and libraries. According to the OCLC report (2003: 31), this leaves LIS professionals with a couple of challenges, such as shifting internal resources to maintain and increase services in the face of static or declining funding, looking at alternatives for funding, using technology to serve more people and deliver more services, and in demonstrating and increasing the economic value of libraries.

Technology landscape

With regard to the technology landscape, the report notes the need to bring structure to unstructured data, to use distributed component-based software, to move to open source software and to consider the issues of security, authentication and digital rights management (DRM). Libraries therefore need to figure out how to take advantage of these new technologies and new architectures to deliver new or additional services. They also need to work together to build more open source solutions, as well as in looking for DRM solutions.

Research and learning landscape

In the research and learning landscape, the report notes reduced funding for libraries, the proliferation of e-learning, a stronger emphasis on lifelong learning in the community, and changing patterns of research and learning in higher education. There is also the increased importance of institutional repositories, scholarly communication and open access, and new flows of scholarly materials to be noted.

The report therefore suggests that libraries should consider points of contact between libraries, museums, public service, broadcasting and education as well as for ways of aligning themselves with the e-learning communities. Another opportunity might be to look at the support required for an informed citizenery and creating learning and creative opportunities. Libraries should also consider their organisational structures and the need to reconsider library education in the light of these changes. Another issue is the preservation of digital collections and access to these.

Library and professional landscape

For the library landscape the OCLC (2003) report noted major trends with regard to staffing, new roles, the need to accommodate users, the issue of traditional versus non-traditional content, the need for preservation and persistence, and the issues of funding, accountability and collaboration. The report states: 'We're well aware of trends and issues but many staff are not truly willing to change the way they do things' (OCLC, 2003: 73).

For each of the landscapes, the major implications for libraries and information service providers are explored, highlighting the following aspects: an increasingly interconnected environment, the need for systems support, a growth in formalised sharing, a need for new repository and content standards, and the emphasis on universal access to information.

By monitoring the professional landscape, we can prepare to react to changes, but also to take a direction to initiate such changes. A number of things can, for example, be noted, such as new career paths, conferences where we can present papers, network and be seen, how we can get professionally involved (e.g. by writing columns, articles, books and book reviews), and the difference we can make in the services we offer and the value we add. We can also offer presentations based on the trends noted – to name but a few.

A specialised field: indexing

Instead of taking a more holistic view of the environment, one can focus very narrowly on one's field of specialisation – I have previously referred to this as a micro-world view. Except for very small and solo libraries, most LIS professionals have some focus point, such as cataloguing, reference work, consortia or information literacy. So many possibilities and exciting things are happening in each of these specialised fields, that even in this narrower field, we need to be selective in what we monitor. In this section I will briefly look at some of the aspects that might be monitored if you specialise in indexing (the list is not intended to be exhaustive). The following seems to be of importance to indexers:

- new publications, such as books on indexing, reference works, and also books on information organisation, information seeking and information retrieval;

- articles and conference papers on aspects concerning indexing;

- reference sources (especially those freely available via the Web);

- standards and guidelines affecting indexing;

- information concerning publishers;

- developments concerning Internet searching and indexing;

- conferences, courses, workshops;

- indexing awards;

- developments concerning professional associations;

- salary comparisons;

- fees and contracts for indexers;

- indexing software;

- job opportunities;

- new discussion lists;

- developments in the publishing and editing industries.

General alertness

There are many things to notice as a good citizen. Things that come to mind are terrorism, war, natural disasters and preparing for these, as well as local, national and international politics. There are, for example, heated debates about privacy of information and increased security measures taken by governments. It is unarguable that you should take note of these, at least through watching the news and reading newspapers. How much time, however, is it worth your while to get involved in these hectic debates? If you have your mind set on making a difference and changing laws, then go for it. If, however, you merely intend to be an opinionated onlooker, it is perhaps a good idea to ask yourself how much time you should spend on this, and whether there are other issues of society and your career that need your attention more urgently.

Similarly, LIS professionals who are informed about the weather patterns, sport teams, cricket scores, financial fluctuations and political intricacies are always a pleasure to talk to. But how much does this add to your career path and opportunities, and how much time should you spend on this – especially office time? LIS situations where it is important to notice these things are public and school libraries (e.g. by offering timely displays on tsunamis) or showing a wide general knowledge to the patrons of the public library.

To be successful in our careers, we need to be well-balanced people with a social life and time for relaxation. If we wish to be alert in our jobs, we should realise that we need to find a fine balance in the type of information that we monitor. My advice would be that general alertness should not exceed your alertness to the professional environment – especially not if this 'alertness' is gained during office hours. Personal time can of course be spent according to personal preferences.

A benchmark for LIS professionals

If we as LIS professionals want credibility among other professionals, we should trust our own services and products in staying abreast. I would expect a sales consultant in a boutique to be well dressed with immaculate taste. I would expect a financial broker to do well financially, as I would expect an academic to set an example to students in terms of research output. Although many LIS professionals are using alerting services for their own use, I am not aware of any that can be 'benchmarked' in terms of the scope of monitoring or putting information to use.

The concept of benchmarking is mostly linked to organisations and institutions and quality management techniques. In the context of benchmarking information management activities, Wilson and Strouse (2005) describe benchmarking as 'a process for comparing operations and strategies among peer groups. It allows participants to identify best practices, rationalise resources, and generally ensure that they are providing top value to their organisations relative to peers in other organisations or functions'. Skills can be honed by means of benchmarking, and quality and ongoing continuous innovation, improvement and learning can be promoted (Carpenter and Rudge, 2003; Wilson and Strouse, 2005). In a very extensive literature review on benchmarking, Dattakumar and Jagadeesh (2003) cite an article on benchmarking for change management as well as an article on benchmarking for career management. Perhaps it is time to consider the benchmarking of alerting services aimed at making a professional difference.

Conclusion

In this chapter I considered the different approaches to the professional and wider environment to be monitored. Nobody can monitor everything, and therefore we need to take informed decisions of what part of the environment to monitor and where we should start. In doing so, our intentions in using alerting services and our personal preferences and abilities will play a major role. Within a highly dynamic world there is much more to note than any one person can manage; cooperation with peers and colleagues and environmental scanning by professional organisations therefore becomes very important. After carefully considering the potential environment to monitor and some brainstorming and mind-mapping about our intentions, personal preferences, and how we look at the environment, we should be able to come up with:

- a mind map reflecting our information needs and urgency to stay abreast (this will be our information needs profile); and

- a mind map of our situation in the larger environment, linked to our personal preferences and intentions for using alerting services; this should be based on an assessment of our strengths, weakness, opportunities and threats (i.e. a SWOT analysis).

This will serve as basis for the selection of alerting services that will be used. Such services are discussed in the next chapter.

A final thought: to ensure that our use of alerting services can serve as an example to other professionals, it is perhaps time to benchmark our efforts, and to start with in-depth studies of the information needs and information seeking of LIS professionals with regard to alerting services.

Available alerting services

Introduction

Many Web-based services can be used to stay abreast of developments. The wonderful thing, as already mentioned, is that many of these are available for free. Often they are speedy and convenient to use. They commonly give access to information that is not readily available elsewhere, for example, conference calls for papers and journals available in electronic format only. Alerting services are no longer only available to those who can afford them. This also means, however, that we have no excuse for not keeping track of our core business.

Traditionally we mostly think of alerting services in terms of types or methods, for example, tables of contents, journal circulation, acquisitions lists, indexing and abstracting journals, and current awareness lists of publications, such as the *Journal of Academic Librarianship* guide to the professional literature. Many other journals also offer a limited alerting service, such as *The Electronic Library* and *Current Awareness Abstracts* (ASLIB).

Different types of alerting services are available, as will be discussed in the following sections. Although examples of services relevant to LIS professionals are noted, the intention is not to offer an exhaustive list. As Nesbeitt and Gordon (2002: 52) explain: 'These days, it can be said that keeping up with even current awareness resources in the information profession has become an issue'.

Furthermore, Web alerting services can and should be supplemented by using traditional methods, such as scanning the bookshelves of the library or bookshop, leafing through journals, listening to the television and radio news, talking to colleagues at conferences and workshops, and making new professional acquaintances.

Exploring as widely as possible

Some people suggest that LIS professionals should use only a single source to keep up to date and avoid information overload, as well as such levels of frustration that one would rather choose not to be alert at all (Cohen, 2003). If one merely wishes to note a few key developments, this is certainly the way to go. If, however, you wish to survive and seize new opportunities even when there is only a hint of them, I believe it pays to scan the environment as widely as possible, and to focus more on techniques for filtering information according to personal insights and preferences. Instead of limiting the resources we scan, we should rather improve on our information processing skills. How can we deal with large amounts of new information? How can we learn to be innovative and creative? How can we improve our lateral-thinking skills? How can we collaborate in using alerting services?

The point of departure of this book is therefore to use sources to stay alert according to your individual situation (as explained in the previous chapter) and your abilities to put the information to use.

Being alert can be achieved through:

- *formal recorded sources*, such as journal articles, books, conference papers, information posted on websites, and the like;

- *formalised personal sources*, such as discussion lists, weblogs, conference papers, workshops, training sessions, and the like;

- *informal discussions* with people, informal chats at conferences, and the like.

No alerting service, not even very expensive commercial services, will cover all sources of new information, all types of information, or all topics that you might be interested in. This is especially true if you need to cover a multidisciplinary field, or if you are monitoring information for more than one purpose, for example, furthering your career, noticing new trends that might open opportunities, and improving your service to users. A LIS professional working on information literacy programmes might, for example, be expected to cover library science, information science, education, instructional design, information technology, copyright and legal matters concerning LIS, and, of course, any developments that concern the Internet. It would be a good idea to cover new books in the field, journal articles reporting research findings, opinion papers, conference papers, adverts for new products, calls for conference papers, training sessions, new developments concerning databases, what other people are offering on the Web, training materials available on the Web, what key people in the field are doing, and so on – this covers a very wide spectrum. In the previous chapter we considered what indexers should monitor, which also covered quite a spectrum.

When thinking about using alerting services, the question should not purely be how much time it will take to cover such a spectrum, but how we can benefit. In addition, how much time does it take to monitor developments in comparison with coming up with our own solutions?

In addition to what we have already said about monitoring the environment in the previous chapter, one should also decide whether to monitor theoretical information or purely information for the practitioner. I would opt for both, because the gap between LIS theory and LIS praxis has been a cause for concern for many decades. The result is that theory seldom finds its way into praxis, thus nothing is changing, and we are not as good as our theory indicates we should be, because we don't learn from our own theory. We might not even be aware that the theory exists! There is also the other side of the coin. If academics and researchers do not monitor practical developments through the literature aimed at practitioners, they might not even be aware of concerns in praxis.

It is therefore suggested that LIS professionals should monitor as wide a spectrum as possible, but should also be:

- noting services that might be useful and searching for additional services;

- starting out modestly (one or two aspects/sources initially); first see what and how much you can manage (as stressed in the previous chapter);

- ensuring that they have time to react on at least some of the aspects that they are monitoring;

- ensuring that they get professional satisfaction from their efforts;

- bearing in mind all other criteria for the selection of alerting services that will be discussed towards the end of this chapter.

Types of services available

Many of the Web alerting services build on traditional services such as the circulation of journals' tables of content, lists of new acquisitions, personal notification of publications of interest, abstracting bulletins, and so on. There are also some services that are unique to the Web.

The following types of service will be briefly discussed in this chapter:

- websites specialising in alerting services to LIS professionals;
- tables of contents and tables of content alerting services for journals;
- book announcements and online bookshops;
- electronic newsletters;
- discussion lists or electronic mailing lists;
- article alerting services, including selective dissemination of information (SDI);
- weblogs;
- information monitoring and automated tracking tools;
- websites with newsworthy content, including job recruitment, conference announcements and professional organisations;
- news and RSS feeds.

The addresses of Web resources are also listed in the Appendix.

Websites specialising in alerting services to LIS professionals

There are a number of alerting services specifically aimed at LIS professionals where LIS professionals have developed websites to keep other LIS professionals up to date with new developments. Some of these are available for subscription and some for free. If paying for subscription, it is important to ensure that you are getting value for your money.

Arlene Els offers the Informed Librarian Online (*http://www.informedlibrarian.com*). The Informed Librarian Online is a monthly compilation of the most recent tables of contents from over 275 titles offering international coverage of LIS-related journals, e-journals, magazines, e-magazines, newsletters and e-newsletters. Even the *Mousaion*, an accredited journal from the Department of Information Science, University of South Africa, is listed. There is limited free access to the Informed Librarian Online. At the time of writing, the subscription version was $29 per annum, and students could subscribe for $15. Due to the scope of its coverage, this is an excellent source of information.

There are many websites that offer an alerting service to LIS professionals, but that need to be checked on a regular basis. Only a few will be mentioned here to give an indication of the possibilities. To a large extent, the choice of such sites will also depend on personal and subject-related interest, and the variety of other services being used:

- BUBL LINK (*http://bubl.ac.uk/link/1/librarians.htm*): Offers useful references for various aspects concerning library and information science, such as links to journals and professional associations.

- Internet Library for Librarians (*http://www.itcompany.com/inforetriever/*): Offers useful references to other resources.

- LibrarySpot (*http://www.libraryspot.com/libraries/*): A free virtual library resource centre for educators and students, librarians and their users; it is worth checking on a regular basis.

- Digital Librarian – Librariana (*http://www.digital-librarian.com/librariana.html*): Offers links to a variety of sites relevant to LIS professionals.

- Internet Public Library (*http://www.ipl.org/div/subject/browse/hum45.50.00/*): Provides links to a variety of sources relevant to LIS professionals, including electronic newsletters.

- Library and Information Technology Association maintained by Pat Ensor (*http://www.lita.org/LITAMAINTemplate.cfm?Section=lita*): Provides links to mostly information technology related websites.

- Informationcity.com (*http://www.informationcity.com*): Available for free, enabling individuals to connect with other people for discussion forums, newsletters about jobs, etc. It also offers a newsfeed dedicated to LIS and other topical newsfeeds.

Journal tables of contents and journal tables of contents alerting services

Journal tables of contents (TOCs) and journal tables of contents alerting services (TOCs services) are very well known to LIS professionals and although mostly associated with journals there are also services available for books and other publications. In addition to the typical TOC information, such as the title and author(s), many TOCs also offer a link to the abstracts of articles. This is a useful way of getting some idea of trends in the field, and to see whether it would be worth obtaining the full-text article.

There are two methods of using TOCs, namely through the journal or the journal publisher's website or through a TOCs alerting service.

Accessing TOCs through the websites of journals or journal publishers

To monitor a journal's table of contents, one can either access the website of the individual journal, or work through the website of the publisher. A publisher can either send out automatic e-mail messages to subscribers to their TOCs service every time there is a new issue of a journal, or they can allow users to check the individual journals' websites for the TOCs. The latter is a more cumbersome method as the onus will be on the user to remember to do this on a regular basis. Most publishers nowadays are moving to e-mail alerts and RSS feeds which are offered free of charge. If an e-mail alerting service is offered, users can often select a list of journal titles from the particular publisher in which they are interested. A more cumbersome way would be to visit the individual journal websites to subscribe to the e-mail alert.

To ensure a wide coverage of journal titles, you will, however, need to consult the websites of all key publishers in the field of interest. Setting up an e-mail alerting service for a number of publishers can thus be a time-consuming exercise. Regular checking of journal websites can be even more time-consuming (although bear in mind that you are not paying for the service). In this regard, RSS feeds are very useful.

The TOCs alerting services offered by publishers are very timely, and sometimes articles that have been approved, but are still undergoing corrections, are already available. The tables of content of back issues are mostly also available. To access the full text of a journal article, however, users must either subscribe to the journal, work through a document delivery service, or request the article through a traditional interlibrary loan from another library or information service.

Open access resources and personal archiving may, however, also offer a solution. For example, you can search for articles on Google Scholar (*http://scholar.google.com/*)

Publishers who offer free e-mail notification services that are of interest to LIS professionals include the following:

- SARA alert (*http://www.tandf.co.uk/journals/alerting.asp*);

- Emerald (*http://www.emeraldinsight.com/Insight/*);

- Elsevier Contents Direct (*http://contentsdirect.elsevier.com/*). Special section also for librarians: (*http://www.elsevier.com/wps/find/librarianssupportinfo.librarians/alertingservices*).

TOCs alerting services

TOCs alerting services offer access to the TOCs of journals from a variety of publishers. Each service decides which publishers and which journals they will include, although no service will cover all the journals that might be of interest. You will most probably have to subscribe to more than one service, or supplement a service by subscribing to the TOCs of individual journals or the service offered by the journal publisher.

It is easy to use TOCs alerting services to select the journal titles one wishes to monitor, to edit this list and to link to full-text articles. The latter can be available either as part of your subscription to the service, for example, if you are subscribing to an aggregator service such as ScienceDirect which offers full-text access to selected journal titles, or at an additional cost if you are subscribing to IngentaConnect. With each new issue of a journal, you will automatically receive e-mail with the TOCs.

TOCs alerting services mostly also allow you to run one or more alerts on topics of interest (e.g. broad topics such as information literacy or indexing). In addition to the journal titles you are monitoring, you will also be notified whenever new publications on these topics are added to the database of the TOCs services. Such 'double monitoring' will naturally lead to some duplication, but will also help to ensure that you do not miss valuable information.

Some examples of services include:

- ScienceDirect (*http://www.sciencedirect.com/*): for subscribers;

- EBSCO (*http://www.ebsco.com*): offers free access to Library, Information Science and Technology Abstracts (*www.libtraryresearch.com*).

The TOCs of printed journals can also be scanned. In most cases, however, LIS professionals will not have access to such journals. Exceptions would be LIS professionals working in academic libraries that offer services to LIS departments. Nonetheless, it is much more convenient to browse the electronic versions.

Identifying relevant journal titles and publishers

One problem in monitoring TOCs might be to first identify the journal titles and publishers in your field (and, if time allows, related fields). If you have access to databases such as ERIC and Library and Information Science Abstracts or aggregator services such as ScienceDirect, you can do a broad search on keywords that are of interest to your field (e.g. library literacy, evidence-based practice, indexing). Note the journal titles in which articles appear. Then use a search engine, such as Google, to search for the journal website or the publisher's website. In addition, consult the publisher websites for other journal titles that might be of interest. Gradually you can build up a list of journal titles and publishers that are of interest. It might save time and effort to collaborate with colleagues on building such lists. An alternative would be to subscribe to a service such as the Informed Librarian, and to add only journal titles that are not covered – if any.

There are numerous journal titles that might be of interest, such as *The Electronic Library, Online Information Review, Library Collections* and *Interlending and Document Supply*. My personal recommendation would be that more academically-oriented journals such as *Journal of Documentation, Journal of the American Society for Information Science and Technology*, and *Journal of Information Processing and Management* should also be monitored by non-academic LIS professionals to find a balance between theory and practice. LIS professionals really need to bridge the gap between theory and practice. Similarly I would advise academics to monitor journals of a more practical nature such as *Library Hi Tech* and *Searcher: The Magazine for Database Professionals*.

General lists of journal titles that might be of interest to LIS professionals and that can be used to identify journal titles, can also be found at:

- ALA (*http://www.ala.org/library/alaperiodicals.html*);

- BUBL (*http://bubl.ac.uk/journals/lis*);

- Documents in Information Science (*http://dois.mimas.ac.uk*);

- EBSCO's Library Reference Centre (*http://www.epnet.com/lrc.html*);

- Emerald's List of library and information services related journals (*http://www.emeraldinsight.com/librarylink/journals.htm*);

- Eric Morgan's Index Morganagus (*http://sunsite.berkeley.edu/~emorgan/morganagus*);

- Information Research (*http://www.shef.ac.uk/~is/publications/infres/subguide/infres/subguide.html*);

- LookSmart's FindArticles.com (*http://www.findarticles.com/PI/index.jhtml*);

- Librarian's Online Warehouse (*http://libsonline.com/publish.asp*);

- MagPortal.com (*http://www.magportal.com/*);

- The Haworth Press (*http://www.haworthpressinc.com*);

- The Researching Librarian (*http://www2.msstate.edu/~kerjsmit/trl*);

- University of Michigan's Finding Professional Literature on the Net (*http://www.lib.umich.edu/libhome/ILSL.lib/Literature.html*)

Free access to full-text journal articles

Although you mostly need to subscribe to a journal to get access to the articles, some journals offer free access to selected articles (e.g. *Searcher: The Magazine for Database Professionals*), and there are also journals that are available for free in electronic format. The following are examples of journals, which do not only offer access to tables of content, but are available in full text for free:

- *Ariadne* (*http://www.ariadne.ac.uk/*);

- *Bulletin of the American Society for Information Science and Technology* (*http://www.asis.org/Bulletin/index.html*);

- *DigiCULT.info* (*http://www.digicult.info/downloads/digicult_newsletter_issue4_lowres.pdf*);

- *D-Lib magazine* (*http://www.dlib.org/*);

- *E-JASL* (The Electronic Journal of Academic and Special Librarianship) (*http://southernlibrarianship.icaap.org/*);

- *First Monday* (*http://firstmonday.org/issues/*);

- *Information Research* (*http://informationr.net/ir/*);

- *Informing Science* (*http://inform.nu/*);

- *Issues in Science and Technology Librarianship* (*http://www.istl.org/*);

- *Journal of Digital Information* (*http://jodi.tamu.edu/*);

- *Journal of Electronic Publishing* (*http://www.press.umich.edu/jep/*);

- *Journal of Information, Law and Technology* (JILT) (*http://www2.warwick.ac.uk/fac/ soc/law/elj/jilt/*);

- *Library philosophy and practice* (*http://www.webpages.uidaho.edu/~mbolin/lpp.htm*);

- *LIBRES* (*Library and Information Science Research Electronic Journal*) (*http://libres.curtin.edu.au/*).

Starting to monitor TOCs

When using TOCs or TOCs alerting services you could compile a list of journal publishers and journal titles that meet with your specific interests. On the list you can indicate the method of notification such as e-mail or regular checking, otherwise you may forget about the latter. Monitor the TOCs for some time and note whether this proves worthwhile. If not, you should unsubscribe from the journal's TOC. Figure 4.1 is

Figure 4.1 Example of a form to record the titles being monitored and assess the usefulness of the journals

Title	Address	Method of notification	Usefulness
D-Lib magazine	http://www.dlib.org/	E-mail notification	Highly relevant; full-text
Information Research	http://informationr.net/ir/	E-mail notification	Highly relevant
Searcher: The Magazine for Database Professionals	http://www.infotoday.com/ searcher/default.shtml	Regular checking	Reasonably relevant

an example of a form that can be used to keep record of the titles being monitored as well as for assessing the usefulness of the journals.

Book announcements and online bookshops

There are two main methods for noting new book titles, namely through online bookshops or book publishers. Book reviews published in journals, are also very useful.

New books or other document titles, such as videos or CDs, can be identified through automatic notification services from online bookshops or directly from the publishers. Books can, for example, be monitored by specifying broad categories such as 'information literacy', 'indexing' or 'collection building'. Often these services also offer pre-publication titles. For example, this book has been advertised on Amazon since the author signed a contract with the publisher.

Online bookshops can also offer book recommendation services (e.g. based on previous purchases). Only two of the most important bookshops will be mentioned here, namely:

- Amazon (*http://www.amazon.com*);

- Barnes and Noble (*http://www.barnesandnoble.com*).

There are also many country specific online bookshops that you should note.

Apart from online bookshops, new book titles can be monitored through the websites of book publishers. A large number of publishers are of interest to LIS professionals. These include publishers from professional associations such as CILIP and ALA. The following are just a few examples:

- ALA (*http://www.ala.org*);

- Chandos (*http://www.chandospublishing.com*);

- Facet Publishing (Owned by CILIP) (*http://www.facetpublishing.co.uk*);

- Haworth Press (*http://www.haworthpress.com*);

- Libraries Unlimited (*http://www.lu.com*);

- Information Today (*http://www.infotoday.com*).

A highly relevant publication that came from Libraries Unlimited at the time of publication of this book, for example, is *The Next Library Leadership: Attributes of Academic and Public Library Directors*, by Peter Hernon, Ronald R. Powell and Arthur P. Young.

Relevant publishers to monitor can also be identified by using publications such as:

- The Bookwire Index (*http://www.bookwire.com*);

- Directory of Publishers and Vendors (*http://acqweb.library.vanderbilt.edu/pubr.html*).

Similar to the use of TOCs and TOCs alerting services, a list of publishers and book alerting services can be compiled for monitoring new book titles.

Electronic newsletters

Electronic newsletters can be useful information sources. A very useful one, Library Juice (*http://www.libr.org/Juice/*), edited by Rory Litwin, was, however, discontinued in September 2005. One of Litwin's arguments was that it is getting more difficult to find useful themes to write about without repeating what is already available on the Web.

Many professional organisations also have their own electronic newsletters. Sometimes these are available freely, and sometimes only to members. A few examples of such newsletters include the following:

- Current Cites (*http://lists.webjunction.org/currentcites/*): A team of librarians and library staff monitors information technology literature;

- Info Career Trends – Lisjobs.com's Professional Newsletter (*http://www.lisjobs.com/newsletter/*);

- Library and Information Science News (*http://www.lisnews.com/journal.pl?op=top*);

- Mary Ellen Bates' search tip of the month (*http://www.batesinfo.com/subscribe.html*);

- Search Engine Watch (*http://searchenginewatch.com/*).

Discussion lists

Discussion lists, also known as electronic mailing lists, provide the opportunity to share ideas, concerns, and the like with other professionals. They also offer the opportunity to find answers to your questions without searching the formal subject literature. Messages from discussion lists are easy to read and easy to delete. They can, however, also easily clutter an e-mail inbox. When subscribing to discussion lists one should ask oneself, why and how they will be used, and then weigh the value against the effort required.

There are numerous examples of relevant mailing lists. I am mentioning only two, namely:

- IFLA Information Literacy Section Discussion List – InfoLit-L (*http://infoserv.inist.fr/wwsympa.fcgi/info/infolit-l*);

- PUBLIB (*http://lists.webjunction.org/publib*).

The following are some of the resources that can be searched to find discussion lists relevant to LIS professionals:

- Mansfield University (*http://lib.mansfield.edu/library.html*);

- Directory of Scholarly and Professional E-conferences (*http://www.kovacs.com//news.html*);

- IFLANET Mailing Lists (*http://www.ifla.org/II/iflalist.htm*).

Article alerting services and selective dissemination of information

Many aggregator services such as Dialog and ScienceDirect offer alerts or SDI services to subscribers. Although subscription can be expensive, it saves a lot of time and effort, and is certainly recommended if your library or information service is subscribing to these services anyway. To use these services, you will need an interest profile.

An interest profile is based on the formulation of a search strategy, for example, '(information seeking or information needs) AND oncology AND nurses'. The search strategy is then regularly run against updates of the service or database.

Examples of commercial alerting services of interest to LIS professionals include:

- Dialog (*http://www.dialog.com*);

- ScienceDirect (*http://www.sciencedirect.com*);

- Cambridge Scientific Abstracts (*http://www.csa.com*).

Alternative, less expensive options such as IngentaConnect (*http://www.ingentaconnect.com*) can also be used.

Weblogs

In writing for *Update*, the CILIP magazine, Hazel D'Aguiar explains:

> I have felt much more up to date with issues affecting libraries ... since starting to read blogs, and have enjoyed being part of a wider community of bloggers, and that is just by commenting ... blogs provide us with a beautifully simple method of developing a global community for the exchange of knowledge. (D'Aguiar, 2003: 38)

Anne Clyde (2004: 2) describes a weblog as 'a web page containing brief, chronologically arranged items of information', or 'a cross between a diary, a website, and an online community'. Clyde's book on weblogs, their use, potential, history and especially their use in the LIS community is excellent, and a must-read for anybody interested in pursuing weblogs.

Weblogs (blogs for short) can be run by individuals for themselves, by professional associations or by organisations on an intranet. Although a blog is usually created by one person, it is possible to have more than one person contributing to the blog. It can be updated at regular or irregular intervals depending on the author's preferences (e.g. every few hours, every few days or every month). The postings (messages posted) appear in chronological order so visitors or subscribers to the blog can rapidly browse new material by date. Postings can have a very personal touch, and can contain information on just about anything. Blogging can be used to comment and report on public issues, the latest news, interesting journal articles, blog pieces, or new web resources. It can take the form of a personal diary, and it can also be linked to items of interest, random thoughts and so on.

Blogs represent one method of keeping up with new developments. They can, however, also be used to capture our insights and inspiration gained through alerting services. In this sense, blogs can be used by individuals or groups to:

- diarise thoughts on new developments, trends, threats, etc. on a chronological basis;
- keep track of ideas and inspirations;
- stimulate thinking;
- keep track of activities to put information to use;
- keep track of a collection of information worth noting;
- add context to pieces of useful information, such as journal articles;
- add links to similar or related articles;
- reflect on the value of information gained through alerting services;
- act as a repository of creativity;
- share experiences;
- allow for alternative points of view and different perspectives (i.e. if more than one person contributes to the blog);

- bring material to everybody's attention that would not otherwise be noted (e.g. local and national events and news that are relevant and worth noting).

Although weblogs can be very useful to stay abreast of developments in a field, it can also be very time-consuming to sift through entries as anybody can publish their view. In addition, it requires the use of special software; Yahoo provides a useful list of such software (*http://dir.yahoo.com/ Computers_and_Internet/Internet/World_Wide_Web/ Weblogs/Software/*).

There are many useful blogs for LIS professionals, for example:

- Search Engine Watch blog (*http:// blog.searchenginewatch.com/blog/*);

- Tom Wilson's information research blog (*http://www.free-conversant.com/irweblog/*);

- Sheila Webber's information literacy blog (*http:// information-literacy.blogspot.com/*).

The following resources can be used to identify useful weblogs:

- Library Weblogs (*http://www.libdex.com/weblogs.html*).

- DMOZ Open Directory Project Library and Information Science Weblogs (*http://dmoz.org/Reference/Libraries/ Library_and_Information_Science/Weblogs/*)

- The Weblog Review (*http://www.theweblogreview.com/ index.php*)

- Yahoo! Directory of Weblogs: (*http://dir.yahoo.com/ Computers_and_Internet/Internet/World_Wide_Web/ Weblogs/*)

More detailed discussions of weblogs relevant to LIS professionals can be read in Blood (2002), Pedley (2004), Winship (2004) and Weblog FAQ (*http:// www.robotwisdom.com/weblogs*).

Information monitoring services and automated tracking tools

Automated tracking tools can alert one the moment a specified website or web page has changed. Such tools are also called website update notification services, information monitoring services or tools for tracking changes. The subscriber to the information monitoring service or the user of the tool is normally notified via e-mail with the changed page attached. Sometimes pages are highlighted to show where changes have occurred (new content that has been added or old content that has been removed).

The following are examples of services and tools:

■ Change Detection (*http://www.changedetection.com/*);

■ ChangeNotes (*http://www.changenotes.com/ index.php?r=www.google.co.za*);

■ TrackEngine (*http://www.trackengine.com/servlets/ com.nexlabs.trackengine.ui.Login*);

■ Trackle (*http://www.trackle.com/*);

■ TracerLock (*http://www.tracerlock.com/*);

■ WatchThatPage.com (*http://www.watchthatpage.com/*);

■ WebSite-Watcher (*http://www.aignes.com/*).

Web pages and websites with newsworthy content

Another more time-consuming way of keeping track of developments is through the monitoring of those websites and web pages proven to have relevant content. The ideal would be to use information monitoring services such as explained previously. Alternatively, the sites should be visited at regular intervals. The following are a few examples of the types of sites that may be useful to LIS professionals.

Job recruiting

There is a wide variety of recruitment websites. One should especially look out for sites for local jobs (e.g. as displayed by local professional organisations). The following are a few examples of recruitment sites:

- Aslib Professional Recruitment (*http://www.aslib.co.uk/recruitment/index.html*);
- Central Library of the Research Center Jülich (*http://www.fz-juelich.de/zb*);
- InfoMATCH (*http://www.cilip.org.uk/jobscareers/infomatch*);
- The Information Professional's Guide to Career Development Online (*http://www.lisjobs.com/careerdev*);
- Sue Hill Recruitment (*http://www.suehill.com*);
- Lisjobnet.com (CILIP) (*http://www.lisjobnet.com*).

Conference announcements

There are numerous conferences relevant to LIS professionals. Such conferences include the fields of library and information science, information and communication technology, teaching and education, etc. Notifications of conferences can offer the opportunity to:

- submit a proposal for a paper, workshop or poster session;

- attend a conference;

- note themes of interest as identified in the call for papers and the programme (even if you cannot afford to attend you can still take note of what is currently considered important);

- note key people, providers, organisations, etc. active in the field (their websites can then be monitored).

The following are a few examples of annual conferences worth monitoring:

- European Conference on Digital Libraries;

- Internet Librarian;

- LILAC (information literacy);

- Online Information and Content Management Europe.

Many resources can be used to trace conferences relevant to LIS professionals, for example:

- UNESCO Libraries portal: conferences and meetings (*http://www.unesco.org/webworld/portal_bib/Conferences_and_Meetings/index.shtml*);

- AllConferences.com (*http://www.allconferences.com/Education/Libraries/*).

Professional organisations

Apart from joining one or more professional organisation (membership is, unfortunately, expensive), one can also monitor the websites of such organisations with regard to information that is freely available. If at all possible, I would recommend that one join local as well as international organisations. The following are a few examples:

- ALA (*http://www.ala.org*);
- ASLIB (*http://www.aslib.co.uk/*);
- Association of Library and Information Science Education (*http://www.alise.org/*);
- Association of Research Libraries (*http://www.arl.org/*);
- Australian Library and Information Association (*http://www.alia.org.au/*);
- British Association for Information and Library Education and Research (*http://www.bailer.ac.uk/*);
- Canadian Library Association (*http://www.cla.ca/*);
- Charted Institute of Library and Information Professionals (CILIP) (*http://www.cilip.org.uk*);
- Health Informatics Society of Australia (*http://www.hisa.org.au/*);
- International Federation of Library Associations (*http://www.ifla.org*);
- SLA (*http://www.sla.org*).

Key issues identified by CILIP for 2006, for example, include desktop searching, enterprise searching, wikis and blogs (moving from broadcast models to participation models), information architecture, taxonomies and the new folksonomy (describing a collection of metadata created by users). With regard to wikis and blogs it is said that: 'The challenge for information professionals is to understand this as a social innovation…' (Anon, 2005).

Newsfeeds and RSS

Newsfeeds and RSS are extremely important in keeping abreast of developments.

RSS stands for RDF Site Summary or Rich Site Summary or Really Simple Syndication. This is an XML (eXtensible Markup Language) tag for a page that allows the content or headlines of a weblog or other news site to be pulled automatically into other web pages or onto your desktop. You can thus monitor postings from various weblogs. IngentaConnect (*http://www.ingentaconnect.com*), for example, uses RSS feeds to keep patrons up to date. The feeds show the latest issue numbers and dates together with a link to the full table of contents at *www.ingentaconnect.com*. RSS feeds can be used to keep track for LIS-related issues or world and national news.

RSS feeds use newsreaders or news aggregators. Numerous newsreaders are available, including freeware, shareware and browser-based options. A useful list of RSS newsreaders can be found at *http://allrss.com/rssreaders.html*. There are free as well as paid-for newsreaders available for download. Once you have installed the software, you enter the addresses of the RSS files that interest you. The program will regularly check these and alert you to new items (Hammond, Hannay and Lund, 2004; Mort, 2005/2006).

Davison-Turley (2005) describes blogs and RSS feeds as 'powerful information management tools'.

Deciding on services

Once you have identified useful services, the next step would be to select the services you intend to monitor. There are many criteria one can consider when deciding on the resources you will monitor. The following are a few suggestions:

- *Coverage in terms of topics and type of material,* such as journal articles, books, websites, conference themes, etc. Also consider the overlap between different services, for example, alerting services offered by ScienceDirect and Emerald, and free e-mail alerts to the tables of content of selected journals. If you subscribe to more than one service, you should expect duplication. The alternative is to ask how much useful information you will miss if you do not subscribe to a variety of services.

- *Costs.* Is the service available for free, or at a reasonable price, or is it a very expensive commercial service that is mostly aimed at the corporate market (e.g. Dialog alerting services or Cambridge Scientific Abstracts alerting services)? Are funds available to subscribe to alerting services, and how much can you afford?

- *Availability and access.* If your organisation is, for example, subscribing to Emerald and ScienceDirect, you should certainly use these services. If not, you need to consider other options such as running an interest profile (e.g. on information seeking behaviour, indexing or information literacy) on IngentaConnect, which is available for a reasonable fee.

- *Convenience of use.* Is there, for example, automatic e-mail notification, or do you need to monitor the sources on a regular basis? Do you, for example, need to go to the bookshop, check the website, or obtain a circulation copy of the journal? Although many journals offer a free e-mail notification service of their tables of contents, there are also many journals for which you have to check the tables of contents on a regular basis.

- *Currency of the information* (i.e. how up-to-date is the information?) Some journals offer access to articles that are still in print, such as *Journal of Information Processing and Management*. There are also preprint services available, such as Open Directory (*http://dmoz.org*). Coleman and Roback (2005) offer an interesting article on the Open Access Federation for Library and Information Science that can enhance LIS professionals' access to their subject literature.

- *Sophistication*. How specifically can you state that you are interested in a complex topic, such as instructional design for collaborative information literacy programmes with students from disadvantaged communities, for example? For Emerald and ScienceDirect you can formulate complex search strategies. These are, however, commercial subscription services.

- *Automatic filtering and recommendation according to your preferences*. Although this can be very useful, it is necessary to ensure that it really meets with your interests, and that is does not take up too much of your time in setting up the initial profile.

- *Ease of setting up your interest profile*. For example, specifying a search strategy or selecting the journals whose TOCs you would like to monitor.

- *Purpose for using an alerting service*. For example, monitoring events, keeping track of trends, new research reports.

Table 4.1 gives more detail on the criteria. It is not intended to be exhaustive, and should be adapted according to individual circumstances and preferences.

Table 4.1   Criteria for selecting alerting services

Criteria	Examples of what you will monitor
Topic(s) (broad category) *These will include all topics that you are interested in*	Information seeking, information behaviour, information searching, information literacy, information needs, qualitative research, alerting services, current awareness services, information monitoring, education of LIS professionals, collaborative learning, collaborative information seeking
Purpose	Noticing what is published on the subject, noticing new research findings, identifying new skills, noticing opportunities for publishing, noticing trends, noticing conference calls for papers, noticing new publications, noticing job opportunities, etc.
Type of information	Events, opinion papers, research reports, case studies, new products, product evaluations, advertisements, comparisons, etc.
Type of publication	Articles, books, news flashes, conference papers, websites, theses and dissertations, book reviews, etc.
Cost	Free, reasonable fee, expensive personal subscription, expensive institutional subscription
Availability and access	Web, individual monitoring, through subscription only, e-mail notification, etc.
Currency of information	Hourly, daily, weekly, monthly, etc.
Automatic filtering and recommendation	Based on purchases of e.g. books, based on choice of websites or links followed, etc.
Ease of use	Very easy, very convenient, etc.
Sophistication	Basic search form, sophisticated search form, single words, combinations of keywords

Conclusion

In this chapter we considered the variety of types of alerting services available via the Web. Many of these are available for free. Although there are extensive opportunities for monitoring the environment, LIS individuals should spend sufficient time on finding out exactly what they should monitor in terms of their specific situation and abilities, as explained in the previous chapter. Once a decision has been made on the alerting services that will be used, these should be closely monitored in terms of usefulness and also how the information is put to use.

Although there are many types and examples of services available, the success of these will, to a large extent, depend on our ability to identify and select the most appropriate sources. Much will also depend on our understanding of our information needs and information seeking behaviour. These will be addressed in the following chapter.

Learning from studies on information seeking behaviour

Introduction

Alerting services are mechanisms that we use to collect information according to how we perceive our information needs. Bruce (2005) uses the phrase 'personal anticipated information needs' (PAIN) which he links to personal information management (PIM) and personal information collection (PIC). Some of the kinds of information that we might need to monitor have already been described in previous chapters, as well as the reasons why we might collect such information.

To be successful in using alerting services, it is time to think about more than the available sources and services, the information that can be collected, and the reasons why we have traditionally been offering CAS or alerting services to LIS users. We need to become more aware of how versatile and evolving our information needs will be in a dynamic environment. We also need to gain a better understanding of how complex information needs are, and how difficult it is to determine exactly what we need. Above all, we should gain an understanding of the forces driving and influencing our decisions and information seeking behaviour. What is actually happening with us when we use alerting services? How does this compare with what we have learned from studies on the information seeking behaviour of our users? How can we use knowledge gained from studies on information seeking behaviour to set a research agenda for the use of alerting services? Only if we understand these, can we come up with countermeasures to protect us from information overload, information anxieties and other side-effects that can be expected when using alerting services.

Although this chapter will follow a more theoretical approach than previous ones, I will conclude by taking a pragmatic look at how LIS professionals can prepare for their use of alerting services.

In this chapter, there are two issues at stake:

- aspects that individual LIS professionals should note that can help them to gain a better understanding of their experiences and feelings when using alerting services;

- aspects that the profession at large and especially academia should note in sharpening research on LIS professionals' information seeking behaviour in order to offer more support and guidance for their use of alerting services.

Studies on information seeking behaviour

Studies on information seeking behaviour offer much to deepen our understanding of alerting services. A number of review articles have, for example, been published in *Annual Review of Information Science and Technology* (e.g. Dervin and Nilan, 1986; Vakkari, 2003). More recently, a growing number of studies have also been reported on Web information seeking behaviour (e.g. Jansen and Pooch, 2001; Fourie, 2002, 2003a). In the 2006 edition of *Annual Review of Information Science and Technology*, Foster (2006) reviews the literature on collaborative information seeking, while Fourie (2006) explores what LIS professionals can learn from studies of Web information seeking behaviour. Recently, OCLC (2005) also brought out a report on perceptions of libraries and information resources, including information seeking habits and preferences.

We have deepened our understanding of the information needs and information seeking of users from a wide variety of disciplines, professions, cultural and age groups. We have learned about engineers, chemists, lawyers, historians, children, students and senior citizens, among others. Apart from working and academic environments, a number of studies have also been conducted on everyday life information seeking behaviour (e.g. Savolainen, 1995). It has been noted, for example, that a number of factors influence the choice of information sources, the need for information, and the need for information monitoring, etc. Such factors include the task or working environment, the requirements of the discipline, cultural influences, personality and learning styles. We will look at these in more detail in the following sections.

Hardly anything, however, is known about the information behaviour of LIS professionals, especially their information needs concerning alerting services. We only read about their role in offering information services to users, information literacy programmes, and so on. An exception is the article by Stenstrom and Tegler (1988) in which they express concern about LIS professionals' use of CAS, and Tedd and Yeates' (1998) and Yeates' (1999) descriptive articles on the use of NewsAgent. The question arises: to what extent can we expect the information behaviour of LIS professionals to differ from other groups and what similarities can we expect?

I believe it is time for LIS professionals to start asking questions about their information seeking behaviour, with particular regard to alerting services. For example:

- How do they experience their information needs?

- How do they try to meet their information needs (e.g. bridging the gap)?

- How do their jobs and task environment influence their information needs and information seeking behaviour?

- How do they deal with anxiety related to information needs?

- What feelings are they experiencing when using alerting services?

- What impact do their learning styles and personalities have on their use of alerting services?

- How confident are they about their chances of being successful in using alerting services?

- How interactive are they in their use of alerting services?

- Which stages/phases do they experience in their use of alerting services?

- How often and for what reasons do they change their minds when using alerting services?

- What knowledge do they need and what do they know that will enable them to use alerting services successfully, for example, knowledge about available services, knowledge about setting up an interest profile (i.e. demarcating what they intend to monitor), and so on?

- What barriers are influencing their use of alerting services?

- How do they actually put the information to use? How well are they informed about putting information to use (e.g. writing articles, preparing research proposals, business plans, instructional designs, preparing conference papers)?

In the following sections we will consider some of the aspects that will shed further light on the above questions, to help us to understand how we are using (or not using) alerting services, and why some people are keener to seek and use information than others. There is, however, a much richer literature on information seeking studies that cannot be covered here.

What is information behaviour?

According to Wilson (1999b), information seeking and information behaviour belong to the broader field of user studies. He explains:

> [I]nformation behaviour may be defined as the more general field of investigation ... with information seeking behaviour being seen as a sub-set of the field, particularly concerned with the variety of methods people employ to discover, and gain access to information resources, and information searching behaviour being defined as a sub-set of information seeking, particularly concerned with the interactions between information user (with or without an intermediary) and computer-based information systems, of which information retrieval systems for textual data may be seen as one type. (Wilson, 1999b: 263)

Information seeking can be active or passive. As part of our information behaviour we can decide that we do not want to seek information, or we can be unaware of the fact that we might need information. Active information seeking, on the other hand, includes everything we use to find information. As previously noted, there are a wide variety of alerting services. We can use one or two such services, or a variety of complementary services. Our choices in using these services as well as how we interact with them reflect our information seeking behaviour.

Information seeking has been shown to be complex, dynamic social behaviour. One can do it alone or by interacting with colleagues and peers. Collaborative information seeking especially has become more important in recent years, and is certainly something that we need to explore when making use of alerting services.

Our concept of information needs

Our use of alerting services is directed by our perceptions of our information needs and what we believe is expected from us with regard to our jobs, etc. – as Bruce (2005) puts it: our PAIN. The concept of 'information needs' seems to be straightforward and something we can easily explain. However, it is actually much more complicated. 'Information needs', for example, has been described as experiencing a gap in making sense of a particular situation (Dervin, 1999) and an anomalous state of knowledge (ASK) that needs to be fulfilled (Belkin, Oddy and Brooks, 1982a, 1982b). In both explanations there is a gap between what we know and what we need to know to solve a problem, to make a decision, to give an answer or just to make sense of our world and what we are doing. To bridge this gap, people need information. In the case of alerting services, this is even more complicated, because we need to bridge a gap between what we know (our existing knowledge or our state of knowledge at a particular point in time), and our guess of what we should monitor to be able to bridge a gap that *may* arise at some future point in time, as well as what we think we should know to survive and prosper in a competitive professional world.

From the LIS research literature we have learned the following about information needs:

- People in the same situation will interpret their information needs very differently.

- It is sometimes extremely difficult to understand one's information needs and to express and translate this into words so that one can search for information. Indeed, Taylor (1968) explains this extensively in his widely cited article on question negotiation, which is, by the way, a must-read for all reference librarians. Although LIS professionals, and especially reference librarians, should be experts at interviews to communicate information needs and the formulation of search queries and strategies, this still does not mean that it is much easier for them than for other users to pinpoint what they need and to explain this in words.

- Information needs are based on and influenced by anxiety (Wilson, 1999a, 1999b).

- Information needs are secondary to other needs, such as physiological, cognitive and affective basic needs (Wilson, 1981). According to Rouse and Rouse (1984: 129): 'Humans seldom seek information as an end in itself. Instead, information seeking is part of the process of decision making, problem solving or resource allocation'. When using alerting services, our basic need is professional survival and prosperity. Noting the latest information may help us in this, but there is no guarantee.

The need for information can be conscious or unconscious. In order to find the information you need, there must be a conscious experience of the information need that leads to conscious efforts to find information. In order to use alerting services, we first need to become conscious of the fact that we need information to make a difference to our professional lives, and that we should take active steps to monitor the information that may make a difference (e.g. by subscribing to a selection of alerting services or talking to a colleague).

When using alerting services, our perceptions of information needs will be extremely important in how we attempt to use such services – as also explained in Chapter 3.

Efforts to bridge the 'gap'

Dervin propagates a sense-making approach to information needs and information seeking (Dervin and Nilan, 1986; Dervin, 1999). Users need information to make sense of problem situations. To make sense of a particular situation, they need to identify the gap between what they know and what they need to know. Steps, such as seeking for information, are then taken to bridge the gap, which will lead to an outcome such as a solution to the problem, a decision or a proposal.

We have learned a number of things about how such a gap is bridged:

- People will use different ways and means to bridge the gap they are experiencing – even if they find themselves in similar job situations.

- Sometimes people may even be unaware of the gap.

- If people think the gap is too big, they may be so overwhelmed, that they decide not to take any steps at all to bridge it. This is one of the reasons why we should start modestly when using alerting services for the first time, as suggested in Chapter 3.

Information needs and task performance

Information needs can be linked to tasks and task performance. This is explained in an extensive review by Vakkari (2003), as well as reports by Byström and Järvelin (1995) and Vakkari (1998, 1999, 2001). The type of task has an impact on information seeking behaviour, how the need is seen, the pressure to be successful and the efforts that will be made to fulfil the underlying information needs.

LIS professionals should thus be aware that their perceptions of the task at hand will also influence their interpretation of their information needs, and probably their perseverance in finding information. This can also be linked to other factors, such as demands from the professional environment, motivation, and so on.

As shown in Chapter 3, the professional and work environment will have a very strong impact on our information needs and information seeking behaviour.

Impact of anxiety

During the information seeking process, different levels of anxiety may be experienced at different stages. Wilson et al. (2002) explain:

In moving through each of the stages of *problem identification*, *problem definition*, *problem resolution* and

105

solution presentation, uncertainty must be reduced and individuals are seen as engaging in interaction episodes with information sources (including people and other sources, as well as information retrieval systems) to resolve their uncertainty. (Wilson et al., 2002: 705)

From the research literature we have learned the following:

- It is quite normal to experience anxiety when seeking information.

- You can feel anxious about the information you need and what you should focus on (in the case of alerting services, it will be the information that you need to monitor).

- Different levels of anxiety and frustration are experienced at different stages of the information seeking process. Sometimes people feel very anxious about their choice of information sources, their search topics and keywords, and whether the sources are relevant. Often anxiety decreases when they find information, but it can also increase when people feel uncertain about how to use the information, and how to interpret and apply it.

If you, as a LIS professional, experience any such anxieties – welcome to the 'real' world of the users of libraries and information services. And why would you expect not to feel anxious?

As explained before, the need to use alerting services to seize opportunities in professional survival, can, to some extent, be a stressful situation. In this sense, it might be worthwhile to further explore Miller's theory of monitoring and blunting in which she focuses on how people deal with information under stressful situations (Baker, 2005; Miller, 1987). 'Monitors' prefer to collect information and keep track of developments, while 'blunters' avoid information.

Importance of feelings and emotions

In her research, Carol Kuhlthau (1991, 1994, 2004) learned that the finding of information is not just about how well the information retrieval system or database is performing, or about our knowledge of the topic, database, search techniques, and so on. The search process is also laden with feelings and emotions: frustrations at not finding the right information, or finding too much or too little information. It is laden with joy at making progress, and excitement about what we have found and how we are going to use it. It is also, however, laden with despair about not being able to use information successfully. People can be optimistic or pessimistic about their information seeking. They can believe that they will be successful or they can be very doubtful. These are all very common feelings which are actually also part of all learning experiences.

Information often leads to new questions, and uncertainty about whether the information is reliable or sufficient to solve the problem. Often users find that if they continue with the search and explore different or new options, they get to a point where they feel confident again – or sometimes even more confused. Negative feelings can especially disrupt information seeking and use (Nahl, 2005).

In using alerting services we need to move from becoming aware of information to alertness and the ability to put the information to use in good time – remember the idea is to seize opportunities. In the use of alerting services, we should therefore expect to have strong emotional experiences. The 'ups' and 'downs' mentioned here can be expected to be a normal part of the daily lives of anybody using alerting services – if their aim is to put the information to use.

Personalities and learning styles

Heinström (2003), Limberg (1999), Ford et al. (2002) and Ford, Miller and Moss (2002), among others, have found that personality types and learning styles influence information seeking styles. According to Limberg (1999), learning style and personality can influence relevance judgments, document selection criteria, ways of dealing with information overload, thoroughness in information seeking and decisions to terminate a search, critical information judgment, ways of dealing with bias, search strategies, use of information sources and the effort invested in seeking information.

A number of learning styles have been defined. 'Deep divers', for example, dive deeply into the information flow, and go for depth and quality in choosing information. 'Instrumental' or 'surface' learners tend to memorise and reproduce information, while 'strategic' learners tend to do a bit of both (Heinström, 2003). There are also the unmotivated non-information seekers, the 'lone rangers' who prefer to work on their own, the 'confident collectors' who trust their own abilities to find information, and the 'hunters' who have refined their strategies in coping with information. This can also be related to our behaviour in using alerting services.

As for personality types, the research by Heinström (2003) has, for example, shown that there is a link between a conscientious personality and strategic approaches to learning. Such people will display orderly and systematic search behaviour, they will put in much effort, will use a number of sources, will plan their searches in advance, and will be able to judge the relevance of documents with confidence.

Open personalities have shown that they are looking for new ideas and challenges in their information behaviour and that they have a high critical ability.

The question is: how can we apply this to understanding information behaviour when using alerting services? How can we learn more about ourselves and our learning styles?

Impact of self-efficacy

Bandura (1997) formulated the theory of self-efficacy. Self-efficacy concerns our beliefs in our abilities to be successful, for example, in finding information. It has been proven to have an impact on information seeking behaviour (Waldman, 2003). Self-efficacy beliefs will determine how long we persist in information seeking, and indeed whether we engage in the task at all. Self-efficacy beliefs have a major impact on the use of alerting services, as it can be very easy to despair if we do not believe in our abilities to successfully use information collected through alerting services to seize new opportunities. Phrases such as 'dying for information', 'information anxiety' and 'information related diseases' can be found in the subject literature and are real concerns of modern society.

In previous sections we have indicated that anxiety and negative feelings are normal in information seeking, and should be expected when using alerting services. If accompanied by low levels of self-efficacy they can, however, lead to serious negative experiences.

Interactivity and dynamics of information seeking

Information seeking is an interactive, iterative, cyclical and dynamic process. Complex information needs may consist of more than one 'information need', and may often require more than one episode of information seeking (Bryström and Hansen, 2002: 246). Our information needs can change as we interact with the information services and the actual information. When using alerting services, we should actually expect our needs to change constantly. We therefore need to be prepared to adapt our search strategies and our choice of services. This is especially important in monitoring information in a very dynamic environment.

Different phases of information seeking

Different phases, stages and moves have been identified in information seeking. Kuhlthau, (1991, 1994) refers to initiation, selection, exploration, formulation, collection and presentation, while Choo, Detlor and Turnbull (2000) distinguish starting, chaining, browsing, differentiating, monitoring and extracting. Some information seekers, for example, engineers, have shown a change in their preferences for information sources depending on their phase of information seeking (Ellis, 1989; Ellis and Haughan, 1997); in certain phases information monitoring (i.e. using alerting services) features more strongly.

When using alerting services, our focus is on information monitoring, but this does not mean we cannot return to the other phases. For example, before making a final decision or setting out to 'seize opportunities', we can do a retrospective search to learn more about a particular topic or trend that has been noted through alerting services.

It is normal to change your mind

From research efforts it seems 'normal' for users not only to change and adapt their information needs and information strategies, but also to change their minds about the relevance of documents and what information they actually require. Spink (1997), Spink, Bateman and Greisdorf (1999) and Cosijn and Ingwersen (2000) deal with different aspects of relevance judgment. Much also depends on evolving cognitive structures, personality, learning styles, and so on. When using alerting services it is especially important to realise that if we wish to stay in front, we constantly need to reconsider our decisions and 'change our minds'.

Importance of knowledge

In the well-known cognitive model of information retrieval, Ingwersen (1992) and, more recently, Ingwersen and Järvelin (2005) emphasise the understanding of various components of an information retrieval system. These include an understanding of the records in databases, the abstracts for articles, the vocabulary used, how the systems or services operate, the techniques that can be used, and so on. These are all important when using alerting services, as is the ability to set up an interest profile for the diverse topics, document types, etc. you intend to cover. Knowledge of putting information to use is especially important. In the following chapter we will consider some aspects in this regard.

Barriers to successful information seeking

A number of barriers that impact on information seeking behaviour have been identified through empirical research.

Such barriers will probably also impact on the use of alerting services, and therefore need to be noted.

Barriers to information seeking include the following:

- Barriers related to the occupation and task environment: demands and expectations from the job, task complexity, company ethos and work patterns, discipline in which the occupation falls, and so on.

- Barriers related to the information seeker: cognitive style, learning style, personality, experiences with information seeking and information retrieval systems, research skills, conceptual understanding of the topic(s) and/or problem, computer literacy, training received, psychological factors, gender, age, motivation, and so on.

- Barriers related to the information retrieval systems (e.g. alerting services): the intuitiveness of the systems, the sources available, and so on (Byström, 2002; Byström and Järvelin, 1995; Kim and Allen, 2002; Large, Beheshti and Rahman, 2002; Lazonder, Biemans and Wopereis, 2000; Pennanen and Vakkari, 2002; Schamber, 2000; Wilson, 1999a; Wilson et al., 2002).

Wilson (1999a) also explores stress/coping theory (which offers explanations for why some needs do not invoke information seeking behaviour); risk/reward theory (which may help to explain which sources of information may be used more than others by a given individual), and social-learning theory (which embodies the concept of self-efficacy, that is, the idea that one can be successful).

Putting information to use

Unfortunately, once you have gone through the effort of tracking or monitoring information, there is no guarantee that the information will actually help you to bridge the gap, and that you will take the right decisions, because much will still depend on your knowledge, experiences, and so on (i.e. your cognitive structures).

Todd's (2005) information intents theory tells us more about what happens in people's minds when they put information to use. The same information will affect people differently, it will lead to different feelings, and they will take different measures and decisions. In terms of the use of alerting services, extensive research is especially required on how we put information to use. Some suggestions are made in Chapter 7, but these are suggestions only. We need to do empirical research on what actually happens with LIS professionals – especially with those people who are considered to be the leaders in the field.

Time for information seeking studies on LIS professionals

We might know quite a bit about LIS users and their information needs as experienced in different contexts. It is, however, time to learn more about the information seeking behaviour of LIS professionals, and especially with regard to alerting services. Apart from the aspects mentioned in the preceding sections, it is necessary to look at the following:

- how we can deepen our understanding of alerting services through research inspired by the learning sciences (e.g. cognitive science);

- how we can learn from studies on communities of practice (Davenport and Hall, 2002; Davies, 2005).

What can we do for the moment?

While awaiting research projects and results, LIS professionals need to continue with their use of alerting services. Based on the preceding discussion on what we have learned from information seeking studies, it might be worthwhile to consider the matters detailed in Table 5.1.

Table 5.1 Considerations while awaiting research projects and results

Your concept of information needs	What information do you need to be successful in your job and to benefit from opportunities? (This is dealt with in detail in Chapter 3). Do you know how to pinpoint this in terms of search topics and search terms? What is the main need (e.g. getting promotion, being noticed in the profession) for which the information need is a secondary need?
Efforts to bridge the 'gap'	Do you experience a gap between what you know and what you need to know to be able to seize opportunities? What is the 'gap' that you experience between what you know (i.e. your existing knowledge, skills) and what you need to know? How do you plan to bridge this gap by using alerting services? (Do you have the knowledge, expertise, etc.?) Do you think that you will be able to bridge this gap, even if it may be difficult at first?
Link between information needs and task performance	What does your job/task expect from you in terms of being alert to new information? (This is dealt with in detail in Chapter 3). How much pressure is there on you to note new information? What motivation can you get from your job/task environment? Will there be any rewards for you in noting new information? Is the culture in your job/task environment supportive of the use of alerting services?

Table 5.1	Considerations while awaiting research projects and results (cont'd)
Impact of anxiety	Do you feel anxious about the need to be up to date with new information? How strong is the anxiety? Will the anxiety motivate you to use alerting services?
Importance of feelings and emotions	How do you feel about your information needs and your need to use alerting services? How do you plan to deal with negative feelings? What will help you to deal with your negative feelings? Can you share your positive feelings with somebody?
Importance of personalities and learning styles	How do you like to learn about new things? How do you prefer to search for information? Which information sources do you prefer? What kind of personality do you have (e.g. open to experiences, introvert, extrovert)? How can you learn more about your learning style and personality type?
Impact of self-efficacy	How confident are you that you will be successful in using alerting services? How confident are you that you are monitoring the right information, topics, etc.? How confident are you that you will be able to interpret the information and make the right decisions/moves? If your levels of confidence are low, how do you plan to deal with this?
Interactivity and dynamics of information seeking	Are you prepared for the fact that the use of alerting services requires dynamic and interactive search behaviour? Are you prepared to regularly adapt your strategies and choice of services according to what your circumstances require?
Going through phases/stages	Do you realise that the use of alerting services may also mean that you sometimes will have to do retrospective searches (i.e. searches to establish what has been published on a particular topic)?

Table 5.1	Considerations while awaiting research projects and results (cont'd)
Changing your mind	Will you be able to deal with the fact that you will often change your mind on the information that you need to monitor and how you need to use the information?
Required knowledge	Do you have the knowledge to use alerting services, and if not, do you know where to get help?
Barriers to your use of alerting services	Which factors will influence your use of alerting services? Apart from barriers that have already been mentioned, the following should especially be considered: ■ access to alerting services; ■ time to use the services; ■ motivation.
Putting information to use	How competent and experienced are you in putting information to use (e.g. writing articles, opinion papers, conference papers, plans for new services)? Are you prepared to learn how to put information to use, and to improve your skills? Are you interested in identifying role models and mentors?

Conclusion

Although much can be learned from studies on information seeking behaviour (we only touched on a few aspects in this chapter), we still need extensive research on the information seeking behaviour of LIS professionals, and especially their use of alerting services. If LIS professionals understand their own behaviour, it might also be easier to offer support to the users of libraries and information services.

6

Surviving the negative side of alerting services

Introduction

In preceding chapters we considered the changing concept of current awareness or alerting services aimed at seizing opportunities, the impact of the professional and societal environment, the reasons for using such services, types and examples of services, as well as what we can learn from studies of information seeking behaviour.

Alerting services are, however, not just about positive things and opportunities; there is also a very strong negative side. Phrases such as 'information anxiety', 'dying for information', 'digital dysfunctioning', 'digital asphyxiation', 'data delirium', 'analysis paralysis', 'cognitive load', 'knowledge load' and 'information fatigue', as well as discussions on information related diseases, frequently appear in the media.

On the one hand, there are people who suggest that information overload is a myth, or that it is over-exaggerated, and on the other hand, there are people who feel so strongly about the burden of information overload that they would, as a preventive measure, rather avoid information at all costs.

Regardless of your point of view on information overload, it is something that should be considered by LIS professionals using alerting services. With retrospective or ad hoc searches, you can perform one-off searches to get information. This information may be much more than you can deal with, and could be considered as information overload. You will find a way to deal with this and then move on – it is a one-off or at least infrequent episode of 'overload' and inconvenience. When using alerting services, however, there is a constant, regular bombardment of information – which if considered as too much or redundant, can become a nightmare. The use of alerting services is not just about information coming to you via colleagues, friends, junk mail, e-mail correspondence, database and Internet searching, etc. You are actually making an *active effort* for information to come your way on a regular basis.

In this chapter we will consider some of the problems associated with the use of alerting services and how to deal with them. The most obvious problem is, of course, information overload, which is not limited to alerting services. According to Hanka and Fuka (2000: 280) 'We are all suffering from an information overload that is only going to get worse'. We are living in a society where we are surrounded by ever-increasing volumes of information. Even though we receive only a very small portion of this personally, we still 'feel' the pressure of the volume of information that is available, as well as the pressure of what we might be missing.

Information professionals are often portrayed as the mediators between users and information overload (e.g. Choo, 2000; Zick, 2000). Interestingly, Eppler and Mengis (2004) suggest that until recently, the discipline of management information systems has not dealt extensively with the problem of information overload. Two exceptions are the work by Bawden, Holtham and Courtney (1999) and Edmunds and Morris (2000).

In this chapter our question is: how can information professionals solve their own problems with information overload as well as other problems associated with alerting services? We will start with the problem of information overload.

Dealing with information overload

There are very different interpretations of what entails information overload. For some it is simply the volume of information that is all around us, while others consider it as the scenario where they receive more information than they can handle. There are also those for whom information overload is all the information they may be overlooking or not having access to when they need to make a decision. According to Bawden, Holtham and Courtney (1999: 249) information overload 'occurs when information received becomes a hindrance rather than a help when the information is potentially useful'. With regard to current awareness services, I support the latter.

We can view information overload in different contexts (see Table 6.1).

Recognising the symptoms of information overload

Although people often complain about the burden of too much information, not everybody suffers from information overload. A first step would be to consider whether we are merely complaining because it is 'expected' of us, or whether we are really experiencing symptoms of information overload. Such symptoms include anxiety, unnecessary stress, fatigue,

Table 6.1   Distinguishing information overload in different contexts

In terms of information available	In terms of the information that we deal with
Totality of stored information Totality of newly generated information (generation occurs on an ongoing basis) Information we receive unintentionally Information we are unaware of Information we seek on an ad hoc basis Information we seek on a regular basis (alerting services) Information in our personal collections Information we once noticed but cannot find again	Information we can use in decision making Information that stimulates our thinking Information that expands our understanding Information that confuses and frustrates us Information that makes it difficult or impossible for us to take decisions Information that distracts us

cognitive strain, reduced job satisfaction, and the inability to use information to make decisions.

Identifying the causes of information overload

There are many potential causes of information overload as can also be seen in the different interpretations of the concept of information overload. Most causes, in some or other way, relate to the following:

- availability of information (e.g. at work, everywhere in society, at home);

- quantity of information (e.g. too much, more than you can handle);

- quality of information (e.g. inaccurate, false, misleading);

- distribution of information (e.g. inconvenient and frustrating methods of distribution);

- reception of information (e.g. you are unwillingly receiving the information);

- storage and organisation of information (e.g. cannot find the information again);

- processing of information (e.g. inadequate information literacy skills, inadequate critical thinking skills);

- attitude (e.g. not interested in information, lack of motivation), etc.

Although difficult, it will help to determine the cause or causes of your particular experiences of information overload. Based on this, countermeasures can then be matched to causes.

Countermeasures

A number of countermeasures to information overload are reported in the subject literature. Although valuable, these should all be carefully considered to see whether they address the real cause of information overload in a particular context and situation. For example, if we apply these solutions, will we still be able to reach our goal with the use of alerting services, namely seizing opportunities?

If a particular countermeasure will keep you from reaching your goal, you can do the following:

- reconsider your reasons for using alerting services;

- reconsider how you plan to apply the measure (e.g. limiting exposure to information);

- consider other countermeasures.

A selection of countermeasures is considered in the following sections.

Limiting exposure to information

If the volume of information received seems to be a problem, a first step in dealing with information overload would be to limit the information to which you are exposed. This can include the following:

- avoiding information (e.g. not subscribing to discussion lists, reading the minimum, not using e-mail);

- admitting and accepting that ignorance is acceptable, and that you don't need to know about everything;

- sharing the responsibility for collecting information; you do not need to take responsibility for everything. It is very important that you can trust your colleagues to notice potentially useful information and to share this with you;

- seriously limiting the number of information sources or alerting services you are using.

Although these will all certainly result in having less information to deal with, they may be counterproductive to your reason for using alerting services. Furthermore, one needs to ensure that the problem really lies with the volume of information, and not with one's skills in processing information.

Promoting support for information processing and creativity

Information processing, that is, the ability and competency to deal with large volumes of information, as well as complex information structures, is very important in our daily and professional lives (Simpson and Prusak, 1995). It has, however, been noted that people differ very widely in their ability to deal with information – especially large volumes of information. Problems with information processing rather than just the volume of information are therefore often given as a reason for information overload. It has especially been noted that there are major differences between the amounts of information that people can process before complaining about information overload, as well as the levels of anxiety they may experience.

Eppler and Mengis (2004: 327) made the interesting observation that some studies actually showed that high information load can increase one's processing capacity up to a certain point. Deciding on what qualifies as information overload is, therefore, very subjective and will differ from person to person.

When using alerting services, and especially when suffering from information overload, it is the responsibility of each individual to assess their own ability to process information: can you make sense of the information you receive, and can you put it to use? If our ability to process information stands in our way, we need to admit it and come up with solutions. We should know ourselves well enough to recognise the amount and type of information we can handle at a particular point in time. Instead of monitoring highly academic journals, for example, you may instead choose to focus on snippets of information for the moment so that you can explore opportunities for offering innovative services or displays in your library. Under certain circumstances, employers can also offer support with regard to courses that can improve information processing skills, as well as creating an environment that supports information processing.

When discussing cognitive load theory, Kirschner (2002) gives an interesting explanation of competencies that we should consider when working on information processing skills:

> Competencies can be construed as abilities that enable learners to recognize and define new problems in their domain of study and – future – work as well as solve these problems ... In other words competencies are a combination of complex cognitive and higher order skills, highly integrated knowledge structures, interpersonal and social skills, and attitudes and values. (Kirschner, 2002: 1–2)

This is exactly what we need to make successful use of alerting services, and to deal with one cause of information overload, namely the inability to process information. Both individual LIS professionals and their employers can take responsibility for this aspect. The following are some measures that can be taken:

- Sharpening information literacy skills. LIS professionals should be the experts on this in terms of finding and organising information, but when it comes to writing and processing skills, I am sure we can all further improve. Indeed, information literacy, and especially the higher-order cognitive skills of interpretation, analysis and evaluation, are often mentioned as a counteraction to information overload (e.g. Bawden, Holtham and Courtney, 1999).

- Sharpening our critical thinking skills and higher-order cognitive abilities.

- Sharpening our speed-reading skills.

- Using techniques such as mind maps, memory techniques,

graphs and visualisations to process large amounts of information. Some of these are discussed in an article on mental agility that appeared in *Human Resource Management* (Anon, 2004). Mental agility is proposed as a solution to dealing with the stress associated with rapidly changing environments.

- Creating opportunities for thinking time. Collecting information is not a substitute for thinking and decision making. It should not be kept for outside office hours only.

- Creating an atmosphere supporting creative thinking (even if it is only a tea/coffee break once every second week in a teagarden or quaint little shop).

- Creating a culture of support and encouragement for innovation through the use of alerting services.

- Starting a 'new initiatives in the workplace' chat group at the office, and making every attempt to stop it turning into the office grapevine.

Dealing with stress and anxiety

Stress, anxiety, worry and other negative feelings are symptoms of information overload that can also have a tremendous effect on creative thinking and our ability to process information. Csikszentmihalyi, in his well-known flow theory, for example, suggests 'that being able to organize one's consciousness in such a way that information coming into awareness is congruent with one's goals and self-concept reduces negative psychological activity, including worry' (cited by Kelly, 2003: 1, 120). If one occupies one's time with absorbing, interesting and enjoyable activities it can liberate psychological energy that might instead be 'wasted on worry'.

This is especially important when suffering from information overload.

There are many techniques to deal with stress and anxiety such as relaxing, yoga, or a weekend away. A more appropriate solution would, however, be to ensure that we do not get stressed in the first place. Two key points need to be remembered here:

- There is information that is absolutely essential to your job (e.g. new copyright legislation that can lead to court cases if not abided with, or, in the case of doctors, new drugs with harmful effects). In other words, there are some things you simply have to know. You must be able to deal with this type of overload, otherwise, at the risk of sounding harsh, you should not be in the job.

- There is information that will be useful for your career (e.g. in terms of seizing opportunities), but not essential. If this kind of information causes you stress and anxiety, then you would be best to completely scale down your use of alerting services. Alerting services should add to your job satisfaction and your confidence that you are monitoring information that will strengthen your position. This should bring joy and satisfaction and raise your expectations.

The following are a few practical suggestions for dealing with stress and anxiety:

- *Manage your time and prioritise.* What is essential to do and to know, and what would be nice for your career?

- *Come to terms with what you can do, and what you need to work on.* If you are young and new in the profession, senior people can certainly act as role models. But remember, you cannot hope to compete with them in being innovative and creative in *all* aspects of LIS work, as they have often worked for many years to gain a more holistic picture of the LIS profession. However, there may be many other aspects where younger professionals may be much quicker to identify and seize new opportunities (e.g. initiatives to ensure social inclusiveness or drawing teenagers to the public library, new job opportunities or new skills to be learned).

■ *Find joy and meaning in the information you are monitoring.* If this is not possible you need to reconsider the information you are monitoring and collecting as well as your reasons for using alerting services.

Finding your own solution to personal information management

Many solutions to personal information management (PIM) have been offered in the subject literature. As early as 1978, Martha Williams suggested that LIS professionals teach their users to design their own personal databases. LIS professionals certainly have the skills for this in terms of knowledge about information organisation and retrieval. This, however, brings a few issues to mind:

■ *Reconsidering the worth of the information we intend keeping.* Is the information we have collected (e.g. through alerting services and retrospective searches) worth keeping and how do we hope to benefit from it?

■ *Reconsidering the time and effort we spend on keeping and organising information.* How much time and effort should we spend on ensuring that we can find the information again that we decided to keep?

■ *Reconsidering the complexity of our PIM.* How complex should our PIM be (e.g. using personal information management software, bookmarks, cabinet drawers or files) and what should be the level of our information organisation and descriptions? If we are trying to be 'too perfect' in how we do this, it may waste a lot of time and energy that we could have better spent on creative thinking and putting information to use. Do you need a broad idea of the topics/categories of information you decided to keep, or do you need a lot of finer detail on why you decided to keep it, and how you intend to put the information to use?

- Reconsidering the need to organise information for later use. How easy is it to find the information again if you decide not to keep it? Jones (2004) and Bruce, Jones and Dumais (2004), for example, explore the issue of finding relevant information, making decisions on what to keep for future use, and on keeping it in such a way that one can find the information again. They refer to the latter as 'keeping found things found'. When Jones (2004) explores what he refers to as a personal unifying taxonomy, he adds: 'How can we make better keeping decisions? In the ideal, we keep only useful information and nothing else. And this information is filed, tagged or otherwise organised so that it is available later when we really need it.'

Two options for finding information for later use include desktop search software and PIM software.

In addition to the many commercial desktop search software products, there is also very effective freeware, such as Coppernic. Goebel Group Inc. offers a very useful matrix comparing such software (*http://www.goebelgroup.com/desktopmatrix.htm*). Software worth consideration includes:

— Copernic (*http://www.copernic.com*);

— Google Desktop Search2 (*http://news.softpedia.com/news/ Google-Searches-Even-Better-with-Google-Desktop-Search-2-6663.shtml*);

— MSN Toolbar (*http://toolbar.msn.com/*).

A variety of software for PIM is also available. This is also referred to as 'reference management software', 'personal bibliographic management software' or 'personal bibliographic software'. This software can be used for recording and using bibliographic citations (references). Once a citation has been recorded it can be repeatedly used in publications, etc. There is a wide variety of such software available, for example:

— BiblioExpress, the freeware version of Biblioscape (*http:/ /www.biblioscape.com/biblioexpress.htm*);

— EndNote (*http://www.endnote.com/*);

— ProCite (*http://www.ampl.com.au/pc_main.htm*);

— Reference Manager (*http://www.refman.com/*).

More detail on reference management software can be found in Mulvany (2000).

Reconsidering use of alerting services on an ongoing basis

As our situations as well as our interests and abilities change, it is important to regularly reconsider our use of alerting services. It is especially important to consider how much we are gaining through the use of alerting services, if at all, and how much of the information we can actually put to use. If the answer to these is nothing or very little, one can:

■ adapt one's use of alerting services;

■ reconsider one's efforts in putting information to use.

Assessing the quality of information offered by alerting services

According to Simpson and Prusak (1995), much depends on the quality of information (or the perceived quality). We can also work against overload by focusing only on information that is of a very high quality. Simpson and Prusak discuss a number of characteristics of information quality. These include truth (it must be valid and reliable), scarcity (the value of the information as being new/unique), guidance and predictiveness (the way in which the information points the way to action), accessibility (the availability of the information to its potential users), and weight (this is the seriousness of the information, and the need to react on the information).

Finding technological solutions

Through many years of research, a number of possible IT solutions to information overload have been identified and reported in the subject literature. It is, however, often difficult to follow up on what actually happened to these solutions in practice. The following are a few examples of experiments and suggestions:

- WaX knowledge management system. The use of open architecture for managing knowledge is reported by Hanka and Fuka (2000). They made the interesting remark that perhaps the greatest stumbling block to the use of technological solutions to knowledge management and therefore also information overload may be the fact that users are actually looking for psychological support, affirmation, sympathy and judgment as well as feedback in their use of information. In other words, filtering and information management techniques are not enough.

- Intelligent software agents and personal software agents for filtering and recommendation. These can help to block large volumes of irrelevant or useful information, but cannot help in putting good information to use.

- Managing e-mail, for example, through filtering or clustering. Schuff, Turetken and D'Arcy (2005) discuss an experiment on managing e-mail overload by means of a multi-attribute, multi-weight clustering approach.

- Search engines that allow for ranking and filtering of information according to relevance or customised profiles.

- Options for customising search results.

- Experimentation with profiles in information filtering based on the role of context in user relevance feedback (Quiroga and Mostafa, 2002). Building a good profile is, however, still a major problem.

- Experiments with information filtering systems that combine cognitive and sociological filtering (based on collaborative filtering) and integrated with user stereotypes. The latter is based on interaction between users. It was, however, found that even if people are interested in the same topic, their slant and reasons for interest may be very different (Shapira, Shoval and Hanani, 1999: 6)

- RSS feeds as a solution to information overload (e.g. Davison-Turley, 2005; Miller, 2004).

- The use of graphs in decision making (Chan, 2001).

- Federated search engines like MetaLib from ExLibris (*http://www.exlibrisgroup.com/metalib.htm*) where searches can be run against a selection of databases at regular intervals, have also been considered for solutions in using current awareness services (Sullivan, 2004).

Not enough time

We are all very busy, so time might be a problem in using alerting services. One should therefore compare the time spent on using individual services with the value of the information gained by using alerting services. It might also be appropriate to reconsider your time management. According to Hopson and Scally (1993: 3), 'Time management involves setting clear priorities for yourself and making sure that you achieve them. Time is a limited resource, so you have to make choices. When the time is gone, it's gone!'

There are a couple of things to bear in mind when reconsidering your time management, namely:

- be absolutely honest with yourself;

- become aware of how you are presently using your time;

- list all things that are wasting your time (e.g. sharing office gossip, interruptions, postponing work, long lunches, too little sleep);

- prioritise your key responsibilities at the office and in your personal life (i.e. the things that are essential for you to do);

- prioritise the way in which you are using your time;

- set realistic goals for yourself and make sure that you achieve them;

- use a personal organiser;

- create a pleasant work environment for yourself (e.g. your office or desk);

- compile a list of possibilities for saving time or beating time barriers (e.g. using waiting time to jot down inspirational ideas or to read a newsletter or article; combining activities such as discussing work over lunch);

- learn to say no;

- determine your prime time (e.g. whether you are a morning or evening person), and use such time for activities requiring productive and creative work (Haynes, 1987; Hopson and Scally, 1993; Mancini, 1994).

Remember that your solutions to time management need to meet with your personality, style, preferences and circumstances. There are therefore no tailor-made solutions.

Appropriate time management can put you in a better position to benefit from alerting services. In addition you should also consider whether you can afford not to spend the time to use alerting services.

Inadequate opportunities in the work environment

Not all work environments may be encouraging new initiatives, creativity, etc. especially when coming from more junior colleagues. This may inhibit the value of alerting services in making a difference to your professional environment. In such situations, one needs to consider the value of creating new opportunities for yourself outside your work environment, for example, in searching for a new job, learning new skills that you may use elsewhere, and also in being an active member of a professional society.

Conclusion

Although there are many benefits to alerting services, one should also prepare for the negative side and especially for the negative affects of overload. Although technology may offer solutions, such as filtering software and collaborative software, it seems as if our success in using alerting services will largely also depend on our cognitive abilities, such as information processing, our attitude towards our job, our emotions and our personality (e.g. in dealing with stress). Personally, I would opt for improving my information processing skills, and for enhancing my skills in creatively and innovatively putting information to use. In addition, remember to start out modestly when using alerting services for the first time: it is better to ensure that you can put information to use than be too extensive in the 'load' of information you are monitoring.

7

Time to reflect on creative use of information – seizing opportunities and surviving

Introduction

As explained in the introductory chapters, CAS and alerting services initially referred to people becoming aware of new information in their field of interest. In our expanded interpretation, the focus was moved to noting information and putting it to use, for example, in being able to seize opportunities. Among other things, this will imply creative, innovative, and timely use of information. Within the constraints of this book it is not possible to provide in-depth explorations of concepts such as 'creativity', 'creativeness', 'innovation', 'success' and 'successfulness'. However, we need to be alerted to those qualities, steps, attitudes, etc. that may be helpful in using alerting services to really make a difference. We also need to be alerted to the complexities of the human mind, learning, knowledge generation, deepening our understanding and the urgency in putting information to use. Although it is complex, it seems to be worth taking up the challenge. As I have explained before, it is about making a start and exploring our abilities, reaching our full potential, and being happy and successful in the process ... and surviving!

Alert means being aware of changes and preparing to react. As more people have access to information, and therefore the ability to be 'aware of changes', the difference in professional survival will lie in creativity and quick response.

It seems as if creativity will always be some mystery to us. According to Yep (1994) the argument for creativity in the workplace is quite simple:

No matter what your profession, you can't remain untouched by the furious pace of change – a trend that promises only to accelerate. It is no longer possible to seek one 'right' solution to an issue or problem and expect that it will remain in place for a long time. Instead, we must be open to the possibility of many different and constantly shifting answers. (Yep, 1994: vii)

In the introductory chapter, I explained that the use of alerting services need not necessarily result in the world being turned upside down or mind-boggling initiatives – if necessary, we can start on a small scale. Even small, but meaningful contributions and improvements to our jobs or personal lives or in an area that we care about can be a good start. Another thing that was also stressed is that the use of alerting services should not be a burden; it should lead to happiness, joy and professional and personal fulfilment. We should work on exploring and reaching our full potential. This links very well to Csikszentmihalyi's (1991) flow theory, which will be discussed subsequently.

Seizing opportunities is about seeing the potential in information and linking it to your personal circumstances and your own abilities and preferences. It is about moving from description of information to interpretation, knowledge building, forecasting and opportunity spotting. To do this successfully, we need to draw on all fields where we can learn something. Success refers, among other things, to 'favourable outcome', 'accomplishment of what was aimed at', and 'attainment of wealth or fame or position'.

The intention with this chapter is not to provide ultimate guidelines, because I really believe that this is not possible. Rather, it is to pave the way for an awareness of fields or theories that may be useful, as well as an awareness of the need for more in-depth discussion and research on how LIS professionals are using information, and how we can improve. As a conclusion to this book, I will now consider a few actions that LIS professionals may find useful in enhancing their ability to successfully put information to use, namely:

- accepting the need to deal with uncertainties;

- understanding themselves and finding happiness in what they do;

- identifying opportunities where they can put 'new information' to use;

- exploring creativity;

- exploring the power of reflection;

- drawing from other fields of study;

- recording ideas and inspirational thoughts;

- exploring the sharing of information and collaboration.

Accepting the need to deal with uncertainties

In earlier chapters I have already referred to the dynamic and uncertain society, professional environment, and so on in which we find ourselves, and the urgency of keeping track of what is happening. This goes hand in hand with tremendous uncertainty and often also anxiety. The dynamics of modern society and the immense uncertainties that we face in taking decisions about our jobs and careers should not be underestimated. As Phillips (1997) explains:

> We are exposed to more and more information. Perhaps, once, this would have implied more power to control our lives. Instead the more we know, the more we realise how many variables there are, and how uncertain life is. We could question more, but what we tend to do is criticise, feel helpless, or at worst distrustful. In order to deal with, or hack, today's realities, we need to be more aware of how we can surf the waves, not control them, which has been our time-honoured habit. (Phillips, 1997: 1)

Much later in his book he continues: 'Reality hacking is about being able to see the white spaces in life and seizing the opportunities that lie in wait there. The opportunity is not necessarily delineated explicitly, so we have to look beyond what is obvious' (Phillips, 1997: 128).

We need to accept that we have to face a lot of uncertainties when deciding about new opportunities and where we can or want to make a difference. We need to accept that we may make mistakes, and sometimes completely fail. We also need to accept that there is no single right answer or best decision. We also need to trust our own abilities to take the right decisions, and to learn from our mistakes. A first step would be to learn to understand ourselves and our shortcomings and to find happiness in what we are doing. A next step would be to deepen our understanding of our learning styles and learning behaviour.

Understanding yourself and finding happiness in what you do

Happiness is not the ultimate aim of using alerting services, but it can certainly help us in coming to terms with the extra time and effort taken up in using these.

In his well-known flow theory, Csikszentmihalyi (1991) paves the way for finding happiness and satisfaction in our jobs and everyday life. He reminds us that the truest approach to experience ultimate satisfaction and to feel happy and content with ourselves comes from looking within. We need to learn to control our consciousness and our minds. 'Because optimal experience depends on the ability to control what happens in consciousness moment by moment, each person has to achieve it on the basis of his own individual efforts and creativity' (Csikszentmihalyi, 1991: 5).

To a large extent, we decide how we respond to what is happening around us. We cannot always change the world, but we can decide on our reactions. LIS professionals can, for example, despair about the possibility of disintermediation or they can see it as a golden opportunity. Our choices of how we use information and how we benefit from alerting services will influence the quality of our professional experiences. Our choices will influence whether we experience the joy and happiness of having the opportunity to do something new with information or whether we despair.

In the limitations of this chapter there is unfortunately no way I can do justice to the work of Csikszentmihalyi (1991: 5). It is a publication to be read on its own – more than once; to ponder on and to draw inspiration from. I certainly intend to re-read it once I am finished with this book. At this stage, I think it is sufficient to embrace the fact that we need to look for solutions to success and contentment in ourselves. This, however, does not mean that we cannot take note of the practical advice that is often offered in popular publications on success, happiness, etc.

A first step would be to understand ourselves and our rationale for doing things better, and the next would be to figure out what makes us happy in our jobs and where we would like to make a difference.

In understanding ourselves, we can, for example, consider our ambitions and intentions and how seriously we take the need for information and seizing opportunities (as discussed in Chapter 3.) We can also consider our personality type and how this affects our careers, our limitations and shortcomings and the boundaries we need to set for ourselves. Where do you come from and how can you benefit from your past experience?

We also need to figure out what we like in our work, and where we would like to make a difference. Apart from taking initiatives at work, improving services, etc., alerting services should also benefit our professional careers. They can, for example, help you to spot opportunities and develop ideas for reviewing books and websites, publishing journal articles, books or web-based publications or columns (these are also methods to keep yourself informed about developments in your field). The use of alerting services can also point to opportunities to do presentations, getting involved in professional organisations and continuing education or community service (e.g. in presenting courses and workshops). Within these opportunities, however, we need to ask where we see ourselves and where we would like to make a difference.

Exploring creativity

Creativity seems to be a key issue in benefiting from the information noted through alerting services. There are very different interpretations of creativity. According to Yep (1994) it is the:

> ...ability to make connections, to see new relationships and linkages. It is the ability to draw from disparate sources and bring them together – to synthesize them. Creative people pull together ideas, facts, thoughts, and experiences that may have been separate, and integrate these elements into a new whole. Thus creativity is a kind of resourcefulness, a special way of using imagination. (Yep,1994: 2–3)

According to *Roget's Thesaurus* the following words are synonyms for 'creativity', 'productive', 'inventive', 'ingenious', 'fertile mind', 'dreamlikeness', 'visualisation', 'visionary', 'luxuriant', 'bountiful', and 'plentiful'. The big question is, however, how do we become creative?

One small component of creativity is reflection.

Power of reflection

One way of getting a more holistic picture of your professional environment and to come up with new ideas, is to allow enough quality time to reflect (i.e. not just a few moments before bedtime or driving to the office in the morning). Apart from keeping up with information, we also need extra stimulation on how to put ideas to use, for example, reading wider than the LIS field and looking for new applications of LIS knowledge.

In the CILIP's newsletter *Update*, Matthew Mezzy (2004) wrote a very interesting list of book titles for 'reflective librarians'. Containing more than 100 titles, the list has been recommended by LIS professionals and covers practical, visionary, inspiring and challenging texts. Each of these is worth reading and pondering on. The titles include:

- Argyris, C. and Schon, D. A. (1987). *Organizational Learning*. Reading, MA: Addison-Wesley.

- Booth, A. and Brice, A. (2004). *Evidence-Based Practice for Information Professionals: A Handbook*. London: Facet Publishing.

- Feather, J. (2004). *Information Society: A Study of Continuity and Change*. London: Facet Publishing.

- Kolb, D. A. (1985). *Experiential Learning: Experience as the Source of Learning and Development*. New York: Prentice-Hall.

- Schon, D. A. (1990). *Educating the Reflective Practitioner: Toward a New Design For Teaching and Learning*. San Francisco: Jossey-Bass.

- Schon, D. A. (1991). *Reflective Practitioner: How Professionals Think In Action*. Aldershot: Arena.

- Senge, P. (1994). *Fifth Discipline Fieldbook: Strategies for Building a Learning Organization*. New York: Currency, Doubleday.

- Vaill, P. B. (1996). *Learning as a Way of Being: Strategies for Survival in a World of Permanent White Water*. San Francisco: Jossey-Bass.

- Wenger, E., McDermott, R. and Snyder, W. (2002). *Cultivating Communities of Practice: A Guide to Managing Knowledge*. Boston, MA: Harvard Business School Press.

These are only a few of the titles listed. The important message is that we need to learn from other fields if we wish to survive in our profession and if we wish to seize new opportunities. Apart from monitoring information in our fields of interest, we need to read widely and reflectively. Our aim should be inspiration and creativity! We should also make an explicit effort to learn from other fields and disciplines.

Learning from other fields

There is much to learn from the absolute wealth of information published in other fields. To do this thoroughly, however, will take considerable time and extensive research. For the moment, though, we can take our lead from the more obvious fields.

From the theory of emotional intelligence we can learn the importance of understanding ourselves and our emotions: joy, frustrations, anxieties, etc. Learning theories tell us that people are very diverse in how they collect and process information and create new knowledge. Among other things, this implies that we will differ in the opportunities we derive from the same information, and that we need to find our own way of what works for us. From constructivist learning and situated learning theories, the importance of our situation and learning from our experience becomes clear. If you are not successful in your efforts, you should learn from your mistakes, and find new ways to be successful. Organisational learning and theories of the learning organisation stress the importance for lifelong learning, collaborative learning, and growing in organisational context. The literature on motivation stresses the importance of both intrinsic and extrinsic motivation. When reading this together with Csikszentmihalyi's (1991) flow theory it is evident that although all of these are very important, ultimately, we decide for ourselves what will work for us and how we react to our situations. From the literature on career planning it is obvious that we need to be proactive and that it is important to determine our strengths and weaknesses. A very inspiring book in this field for LIS professionals is by Nesbeitt and Gordon (2002). Returning to strategic planning, we can learn that it is a way of thinking and not just a set of procedures, which leaves us with the question, how can we change our way of thinking? How can we benefit from social interaction and learn to use the diverse talents and experiences of our colleagues (Corall, 2000)?

There are also many other fields that we can learn from, such as creativity, change management, chaos theory, motivation, psychology, communication, not to mention those that we still need to identify, and which we need to explore for our own benefit. In short, there is still much that LIS professionals need to explore to understand and improve their creative use of information.

Learning from highly successful people

It is always worthwhile to see what we can learn from people who are considered to be successful in their careers. This especially includes people from outside the LIS field.

In an interview with the Franklin Institute Laureates, Adelson (2003) found that they all enjoyed their work, and that they relied a lot on their analytical abilities when they entered new or uncertain fields. 'Their analytical skill allows them to do so with confidence and their creative curiosity give them a taste for it' (Adelson, 2003: 163). They are not scared by uncertainty and chaos – they see it as a challenge and opportunity to be creative.

Scanning through the literature, much can be picked up on the habits of successful people. For example, they tend to:

- be proactive;
- begin with the end in mind;
- put first things first;
- think win–win;
- seek first to understand and then to be understood;
- synergise – they believe the whole is greater than the parts;
- seek for ongoing improvement;
- ask unusual questions;
- distinguish between important and unimportant;
- create a large number of ideas;
- realise that humour and playfulness are often also associated with creativity (Yep, 1994: 3);
- cultivate a future rather than a present mindset;
- get used to moving from the known to the unknown (Convey et al., 1998);
- be persistent.

Successful people are also mindful about the following:

- avoiding procrastination at all cost – according to Mancini (1994), procrastination can be caused by overwhelming tasks, unclear goals, tendencies to over-commit, addiction to cramming, fear of failure, fear of change and unpleasant tasks;
- reconsidering paradigms, that is, reconsidering one's view of the world and especially the LIS world; for example,

one's current paradigm may be based on work experience and current passions;

- understanding the difference between divergent and convergent thinking – divergent thinking is the ability to use imagination to generate ideas, while convergent thinking is the ability to use logic and evaluative processing, such as passing judgment and making a decision on the best alternative (Yep, 1994: 26)

- working on lateral thinking skills – a term coined by Edward de Bono, referring to the ability to think in non-linear, zig-zag directions;

- using the left and right brain – the left brain concerns detail-oriented, verbal, rigid, practical, rational, logical, concrete and scientific approaches, while the right brain concerns holistic, visual, imaginative, flexible, spiritual, emotional, playful, conceptual and musical/artistic aspects (Yep, 1994: 28);

- recognising personal barriers to creativity, for example, insisting on getting one right answer or approach, resistance to change, lack of self-confidence, looking to others to set the tone and make the decisions, and fear of looking foolish or being embarrassed;

- accepting the need to learn and grow;

- realising it is important to deal with disappointments and wrong decisions;

- accepting the need to create ideas and to turn them into opportunities;

- accepting the need to intentionally spend time and effort on looking for opportunities;

- finding and acknowledging one's inner-self (Phillips, 1997; Smith, 1999).

Dealing with all of these in depth, is a study on its own. For the moment it is sufficient to realise the complexity of critical, analytical and creative thinking, the importance of knowing ourselves, and the need to have the courage and motivation to explore our possibilities.

Recording ideas and inspirational thoughts

On the one hand we have the need to be creative and quick in spotting opportunities, and on the other we have the need to record our ideas and inspirational thoughts. Just noting and organising information is not enough. We need time for reflection.

The following may be useful methods of recording our thoughts at the time when we note information:

■ use a scrapbook to write down what comes to mind;

■ draw a mind map to indicate how information from different sources can be linked to a new concept, new idea or new application;

■ keep a professional journal or diary.

We can note ideas, plans, professional dreams, questions that come to mind, things we would like to research or comment on, or new skills we need to learn. Soon there will be a wealth of new information that will leave us with the next decision: what do we use to survive professionally and where would we like to 'seize an opportunity'? This will certainly take extra time and effort, but if we keep our notes cryptic and brief – remember these are for personal use only – they may turn out to be very worthwhile once we start putting these ideas to use, and once we can actually experience the benefits.

Apart from recording our ideas, I would also suggest that we regularly (e.g. once every two weeks or once a month) revisit our notes and reflect about what we have written, and what we did with these ideas.

Another useful method for recording professional reflections is of course weblogs, where we can have an easily accessible electronic record of our inspirations. These can also be shared with others, if we so choose.

Sharing information and collaboration

Over the last few years there has been a growing interest in collaborative work and also in collaborative information seeking. The bulk of research on the latter is reflected on by Foster (2006). Collaboration can be an excellent solution to dealing with the increased workload in using alerting services. This can include collaboration in identifying information resources to be monitored, setting up interest profiles and alerts, sharing the topics and issues to be monitored, and so on. There are, however, a number of issues to consider, such as trust. For example, will all participants pull their weight, are they reliable, do they have the insight to spot useful information, and so on? It is even more complicated when considering sharing inspiration and ideas on how to put information to use, and opting for new opportunities. If the opportunities concern the good of the organisation or LIS services, collaboration may be a good idea. If they relate to promotion of personal careers, however, many complications can be expected, such as competition, and the tendency to keep really important information to oneself.

Conclusion

The preceding sections briefly discussed a few things to consider in putting information to use. If we as LIS professionals, want to use alerting services to survive professionally, to seize opportunities and compete with other professions, there is, however, much more that we need to learn about ourselves, such as the importance of information in knowledge building, our information seeking behaviour and our information needs. We need to understand that there are no perfect solutions: we need to explore what works for us, and we need to move away from the early 'academic' interpretation of current awareness services. The most important aspect, however, is to understand what helps us to be successful in moving on and in making us happy in our jobs.

An added benefit of this kind of knowledge will be that it will deepen our understanding of the users we are trying to convince in using alerting services, and that it may eventually put us in a position where we can benchmark our use of alerting services.

This book has addressed a number of issues concerning alerting services. There is, however, much more to learn, and certainly a wide scope for research from academia as well as praxis. Collaboration in the use of alerting services is certainly one of these aspects.

Appendix: List of Web addresses

ALA: *http://www.ala.org*

ALA *http://www.ala.org/library/alaperiodicals.html* for lists of periodicals

AllConfereces.com: *http://www.allconferences.com/ Education/Libraries/*

Amazon: *http://www.amazon.com*

Ariadne: *http://www.ariadne.ac.uk/*

ASLIB: *http://www.aslib.co.uk/*

ASLIB Professional Recruitment: *http://www.aslib.co.uk/ recruitment/index.html*

Association of Library and Information Science Education: *http://www.alise.org/*

Association of Research Libraries: *http://www.arl.org/*

Australian Library and Information Association: *http:// www.alia.org.au/*

British Association for Information & Library Education and Research: *http://www.bailer.ac.uk/*

Canadian Library Association: *http://www.cla.ca/*

Charted Institute of Library and Information Professionals: *http://www.cilip.org.uk*

Copernic: *http://www.copernic.com*

Barnes and Noble: *http://www.barnesandnoble.com*

BiblioExpress (the freeware version of Biblioscape): *http:// www.biblioscape.com/biblioexpress.htm*

BUBL: *http://bubl.ac.uk/journals/lis*

BUBL LINK: *http://bubl.ac.uk/link/1/librarians.htm*

Bulletin of the American Society for Information Science and Technology: *http://www.asis.org/Bulletin/index.html*

Cambridge Scientific Abstracts: *http://www.csa.com*

Central Library of the Research Center Jülich: *http://www.fz-juelich.de/zb*

Chandos Publishing: *http://www.chandospublishing.com*

Change Detection: *http://www.changedetection.com/*

ChangeNotes: *http://www.changenotes.com/index.php?r= www.google.co.za*

Current Cites: *http://lists.webjunction.org/currentcites/*

Dialog: *http://www.dialog.com*

DigiCULT.info: *http://www.digicult.info/downloads/ digicult_newsletter_issue4_lowres.pdf*

Digital Librarian – Librariana: *http://www.digital-librarian.com/librariana.html*

Directory of Publishers and Vendors: *http:// acqweb.library.vanderbilt.edu/pubr.html*

Directory of Scholarly and Professional E-conferences: *http:// www.kovacs.com/*

D-Lib Magazine: *http://www.dlib.org/*

DMOZ Open Directory Project Library and Information Science Weblogs: *http://dmoz.org/Reference/Libraries/ Library_and_Information_Science/Weblogs/*

Documents in Information Science: *http://dois.mimas.ac.uk*

EBSCO: *http://www.ebsco.com*

EBSCO's Library Reference Centre: *http://www.epnet.com/ lrc.html*

E-JASL (*The Electronic Journal of Academic and Special Librarianship*): *http://southernlibrarianship.icaap.org/*

Elsevier ContentsDirect: *http://contentsdirect.elsevier.com/*

Elsevier ContentsDirect special section for librarians: *http://www.elsevier.com/wps/find/librarianssupportinfo .librarians/alertingservices*

Emerald: *http://www.emeraldinsight.com/Insight/*

Emerald's List of library and information services related journals: *http://www.emeraldinsight.com/librarylink/ journals.htm*

EndNote: *http://www.endnote.com/*

Eric Morgan's full-text Index Morganagus: *http:// sunsite.berkeley.edu/~emorgan/morganagus*

ExLibris: *http://www.exlibrisgroup.com/metalib.htm*

Facet Publishing: *http://www.facetpublishing.co.uk*

First Monday: *http://firstmonday.org/issues/*

Goebel Group: *http://www.goebelgroup.com/ desktopmatrix.htm*

Google Desktop Search2: *http://news.softpedia.com/news/ Google-Searches-Even-Better-with-Google-Desktop- Search-2-6663.shtml*

Google Scholar: *http://scholar.google.com/*

Greg Notess: *http://www.notess.com/*

Haworth Press: *http://www.haworthpress.com*

Health Informatics Society of Australia *http:// www.hisa.org.au/*

IFLA Information literacy section: *http://*www.ifla.org/VII/ s42/index.htm

IFLANET Mailing Lists: *http://www.ifla.org/II/iflalist.htm*

Info Career Trends – Lisjobs.com's Professional Newsletter: *http://www.lisjobs.com/newsletter/*

InfoLit-L IFLA Information Literacy Section Discussion List: *http://infoserv.inist.fr/wwsympa.fcgi/info/infolit-l*

InfoMATCH: *http://www.cilip.org.uk/jobscareers/infomatch*

Information Research: *http://informationr.net/ir/*

Information Research list of journals: *http://www.shef.ac.uk/ ~is/publications/infres/subguide/infres/subguide.html*

The Information Professional's Guide to Career Development
Online: *http://www.lisjobs.com/careerdev*

Information Today: *http://www.infotoday.com*

Informationcity.com: *http://www.informationcity.com*

Informed Librarian Online *http://www.informedlibrarian.com*

Informing Science: *http://inform.nu/*

IngentaConnect: *http://www.ingentaconnect.com*

International Federation of Library Associations: *http://www.ifla.org*

Internet Library for Librarians: *http://www.itcompany.com/inforetriever/*

Internet Public Library: *http://www.ipl.org/div/subject/browse/hum45.50.00/*

Issues in Science & Technology Librarianship: *http://www.istl.org/*

Journal of Digital Information: *http://jodi.tamu.edu/*

Journal of Electronic Publishing: *http://www.press.umich.edu/jep/*

Journal of Information, Law & Technology: *http://www2.warwick.ac.uk/fac/ soc/law/elj/jilt/*

Libraries Unlimited: *http://www.lu.com*

Librarian's Online Warehouse: *http://libsonline.com/publish.asp*

Library and Information Science News: *http://www.lisnews.com/ journal.pl?op=top*

Library, Information Science and Technology Abstracts: *http://www.libtraryresearch.com*

Library & Information Technology Association maintained by Pat Ensor: *http://www.lita.org/LITAMAINTemplate.cfm?Section=lita*

LIBRES Library and Information Science Research Electronic Journal: *http://libres.curtin.edu.au/*

Library Philosophy & Practice: *http://www.webpages.uidaho.edu/~mbolin/lpp.htm*

LibrarySpot: *http://www.libraryspot.com/libraries/*

Library weblogs: *http://www.libdex.com/weblogs.html.*

Lisjobnet.com: *http//:www.lisjobnet.com*

LookSmart's FindArticles.com: *http://www.findarticles.com/ PI/index.jhtml*

MagPortal.com *http://www.magportal.com/*

Mansfield University: *http://lib.mansfield.edu/library.html*

Marcia Bates: *http://www.gseis.ucla.edu/faculty/bates/*

Mary Ellen Bates: *http://www.batesinfo.com/*

Mary Ellen Bates' search tip of the month: *http:// www.batesinfo.com/subscribe.html*

MSN Toolbar: *http://toolbar.msn.com/*

Open Directory: *http://dmoz.org*

Peter Ingwersen: *http://www.db.dk/pi/*

Phil Bradley: *http://www.philb.com/*

ProCite: *http://www.ampl.com.au/pc_main.htm*

Reference Manager: *http://www.refman.com/*

Reva Basch: *http://www.jereva.com/reva.html*

SARA alert: *http://www.tandf.co.uk/journals/alerting.asp*

Search Engine Watch: *http://searchenginewatch.com/*

Search Engine Watch blog: *http:// blog.searchenginewatch.com/blog/*

ScienceDirect: *http://www.sciencedirect.com*

Sheila Webber's information literacy blog: *http://information-literacy.blogspot.com/*

SLA: *http://www.sla.org*

Sue Hill Recruitment: *http://www.suehill.com*

The Bookwire Index: *http://www.bookwire.com*

The Haworth Press: *http://www.haworthpressinc.com*

The Researching Librarian: *http://www2.msstate.edu/ ~kerjsmit/trl)*

Tom Wilson: *http://www.shef.ac.uk/is/wilson/*

Tom Wilson's Information Research blog: *http://www.free-conversant.com/irweblog/*

TrackEngine: *http://www.trackengine.com/servlets/ com.nexlabs.trackengine.ui.Login*

Trackle: *http://www.trackle.com/*

TracerLock: *http://www.tracerlock.com/*

UNESCO Libraries portal: conferences and meetings: *http:// www.unesco.org/webworld/portal_bib/Conferences_ and_Meetings/index.shtml*

University of Michigan's Finding Professional Literature on the Net: *http://www.lib.umich.edu/libhome/ILSL.lib/ Literature.html*

WatchThatPage.com: *http://www.watchthatpage.com/*

Weblog FAQ: *http://www.robotwisdom.com/weblogs*

The Weblog Review: *http://www.theweblogreview.com/ index.php*

WebSite-Watcher: *http://www.aignes.com/*

Yahoo! Directory of weblogs: *http://dir.yahoo.com/ Computers_and_Internet/Internet/World_Wide_Web/ Weblogs/*

Bibliography

Abels, E. (2002) 'Hot topics: environmental scanning', *Bulletin of the American Society for Information Science and Technology* 28(3): 16–17.

Adelson, B. (2003) 'Issues in scientific creativity: insight, perseverance and personal technique', *Journal of the Franklin Institute* 340: 163–89.

Anderson, K. (2003) 'JournalToGo: online medical current awareness service', *Journal of the Medical Library Association* 91(2): 266–7.

Anon (2005) 'Debating the key information industry issues', *CILIP Update* 4(11): 18–20.

Anon (2004) 'Mental-agility training helps CSA staff to manage rapid change... and overcome problems of information overload', *Human Resources Management*, 12(2): 20–3.

Baker, L. M. (2005) 'Monitoring and blunting', in K. E. Fisher, S. Erdelez and L. McKechnie (eds) *Theories of Information Behavior*. Medford, NJ: Information Today; pp. 239–421.

Bandura, A. (1997) *Self-Efficacy: The Exercise of Control*. New York: Freeman.

Bates, M. (2005) 'Search tip of the month', Electronic newsletter (29 December); available at: *www.batesinfo.com/subscribe.html* (accessed: 26 April 2006).

Bawden, D., Holtman, C. and Courtney, N. (1999) 'Perspectives on information overload', *Aslib Proceedings* 51(8): 249–55.

Behrens, S. (1989) 'Current awareness services: in-house methods and commercially available products', *Mousaion* 7(2): 58–75.

Belkin, N. J., Oddy, R. N. and Brooks, H. M. (1982a) 'ASK for information retrieval. Part I', *Journal of Documentation* 38(2): 61–71.

Belkin, N. J., Oddy, R. N. and Brooks, H. M. (1982b) 'ASK for information retrieval. Part II', *Journal of Documentation* 38: 575–91.

Blood, R. (2002) *The Weblog Handbook: Practical Advice on Creating and Maintaining Your Weblog.* Cambridge, MA: Perseus Publishing.

Bottle, R. T. (1973) 'Scientists, information transfer and literature characteristics', *Journal of Documentation* 29(3): 281–94.

Bruce, H. (2005) 'PAIN hypothesis', in K. E. Fisher, S. Erdelez and L. McKechnie (eds) *Theories of Information Behavior.* Medford, NJ: Information Today; pp. 270–74.

Bruce, H., Jones, W. and Dumais, S. (2004) 'Information behaviour that keeps found things found', *Information Research* 10(1); available at: *http://informationr.net/ir/10-1/paper207.html* (accessed: 8 March 2006).

Brunshill, K. (1997) 'The issues surrounding the provision of CASIAS services in libraries', *Interlending and Document Supply* 25(2): 57–63.

Byström, K. (2002) 'Information and information sources in tasks of varying complexity', *Journal of the American Society for Information Science and Technology* 53(7): 581–91.

Byström, K. and Hansen, P. (2002) 'Work tasks as units for analysis in information seeking and retrieval studies', in

H. Bruce, R. Fidel, P. Ingwersen and P. Vakkari (eds), *Proceedings of the 4th International Conference on Conceptions of Library and Information Science: Emerging Frameworks and Methods, 21–25 July 2002*. Greenwood Village, CO: Libraries Unlimited; pp. 239–51.

Byström, K. and Järvelin, K. (1995) 'Task complexity affects information seeking and use', *Information Processing and Management* 31(2): 191–213.

Carpenter, S. and Rudge, S. (2003) 'A self-help approach to knowledge management benchmarking', *Journal of Knowledge Management* 7(5): 82–95.

Chan, S. Y. (2001) 'The use of graphs as decision aids in relation to information overload in managerial decision quality', *Journal of Information Science* 27(6): 417–25.

Choo, C. W. (2000) 'Working with knowledge: how information professionals help organizations manage what they know', *Library Management* 21(8): 395–403.

Choo, C. W. (2002) *Information Management for the Intelligent Organization* (3rd edn). Medford, NJ: ASIS&T.

Choo, C. W., Detlor, B. and Turnbull, D. (2000) *Web Work: Information Seeking and Knowledge Work on the World Wide Web*. Dordrecht: Kluwer Academic.

Clyde, L. A. (2004) *Weblogs and Libraries*. Oxford: Chandos Publishers.

Cohen, S. M. (2003) *Keeping Current: Advanced Internet Strategies to Meet Librarian and Patron Needs*. Chicago: American Library Association.

Coleman, A. and Roback, J. (2005) 'Open Access Federation for Library and Information Science', *D-Lib Magazine* 11(12); available at: *http://www.dlib org/dlib/december05/coleman/12coleman.html* (accessed: 4 January 2006).

Convey, S., Drucker, P. and Bennis, W. et al. (1998) *The Guru Guide: The Best of the Top Management Thinkers*. New York: John Wiley and Sons.

Corrall, S. (2000) *Strategic Management of Information Services: A Planning Handbook*. London: Aslib.

Cosijn, E. and Ingwersen, P. (2000) 'Dimensions of relevance', *Information Processing and Management* 26: 533–50.

Costa, J. (1995) 'An empirically-based review of the concept of environmental scanning', *International Journal of Contemporary Hospitality Management* 7(1): 4–9.

Cox, J. and Hanson, T. (1992) 'Setting up an electronic current awareness service', *Online* 16(4): 36–43.

Csikszentmihalyi, M. (1991) *Flow: The Psychology of Optimal Experience*. New York: Harper and Perrenial.

D'Arguir, H. (2003) 'Weblogs: the new internet community?' *CILIP Update* 2: 38–39.

Davenport, E. and Hall, H. (2002) 'Organizational knowledge and communities of practice', *Annual Review of Information Science and Technology* 36: 171–227.

Davies, E. (2005) 'Communities of practice', in K. E. Fisher, S. Erdelez and L. McKechnie (eds) *Theories of Information Behavior*. Medford, NJ: Information Today; pp. 104–7.

Davies, M., Boyle, F. and Osborne, S. (1998) 'CAS-IAS services: where are we now?' *The Electronic Library* 16(1): 37–48.

Davison-Turley, W. (2005) 'Blogs and RSS: powerful information management tools', *Library Hi Tech* 10: 28–29.

Deardorff, T. C. and Garrison, A. O. (1997) 'Developing an automated current awareness program using microcomputers and electronic mail', *Technical Services Quarterly* 14(4): 1–11.

Dervin, B. (1999) 'On studying information seeking methodologically: the implications of connecting metatheory to method', *Information Processing and Management* 34: 727–50.

Dervin, B. and Nilan, M. (1986) 'Information needs and uses', *Annual Review of Information Science and Technology* 21: 19–38.

Edmunds, A. and Morris, A. (2000) 'The problem of information overload in business organisations: a review of the literature', *International Journal of Information Management* 20: 17–28.

Ellis, D. (1989) 'A behavioural approach to information retrieval design', *Journal of Documentation* 46: 318–38.

Ellis, D. and Haughan, M. (1997) 'Modeling the information seeking patterns of engineers and research scientists in the industrial environment', *Journal of Documentation* 53(4): 384–403.

Eppler, M. J. and Mengis, J. (2004) 'The concept of information overload: a review of literature from organization science, accounting, marketing, MIS, and related disciplines', *The Information Society* 20: 325–44.

Finlay, K. and Finlay, T. (1996) 'The relative roles of knowledge and innovativeness in determining librarians' attitudes toward and use of the Internet: a structural equation modeling approach', *Library Quarterly* 6(1): 69–83.

Ford, N., Wilson, T. D., Foster, A. and Ellis, D. (2002) 'Information seeking and mediated searching. Part 4: Cognitive styles in information seeking', *Journal of the American Society for Information Science and Technology* 53(9): 728–35.

Ford, N., Miller, D. and Moss, N. (2002) 'Web search strategies and retrieval effectiveness: an empirical study', *Journal of Documentation* 58(1): 30–48.

Foster, J. (2006) 'Collaborative information seeking and retrieval', *Annual Review of Information Science and Technology* 40: 329–56.

Fourie, I. (1999a) 'Empowering users – current awareness on the Internet', *The Electronic Library* 17(6): 379–88.

Fourie, I. (1999b) 'Should we take disintermediation seriously', *The Electronic Library* 17(1): 9–16.

Fourie, I. (2001) 'Current awareness services in an electronic age – the whole picture', in A. Scammel (ed.) *Handbook of Information Management* (8th edn). London, Aslib; pp. 274–306.

Fourie, I. (2002) 'A review of web information-seeking/ searching studies (2000–2002): implications for research in the South African context', in T. Bothma and A. Kaniki (eds) *Progress in Library and Information Science in Southern Africa: Proceedings of the Second Biennial DISSAnet Conference* (PROLISSA Conference, 24–25 October, Pretoria). Pretoria: Infuse; pp. 49–75.

Fourie, I. (2003a) 'How can current awareness services (CAS) be used in the world of library acquisitions', *Online Information Review* 27(3): 183–95.

Fourie, I. (2003b) 'A research agenda and framework for web information seeking/searching in South Africa', *South African Journal of Libraries and Information Science* 69(2): 115–25.

Fourie, I. (2004) 'Librarians and the claiming of new roles: how can we make a difference? *Aslib Proceedings* 56(1): 62–74.

Fourie, I. (2006) 'Learning from web information seeking studies: some suggestions for LIS professionals', *The Electronic Library*, 24(1): 20–37.

Fourie, I. and Claasen-Veldsman, R. (2005) 'Disintermediation: using intermediary skills to offer oncology nurses opportunities for their own world wide web current awareness services (CAS)', in J. Gascón and F. Burguillos (eds) *7th Congreso del Capítulo Español de ISKO: La Dimension Humana de la Oganización del*

Conocimento (The Human Dimension of Knowledge Organization). Barcelona: Departement de Biblioteconomia Documentació de la Universitat de Barcelona: pp. 187–200.

Gessesse, K. (1998) 'Internet-accessed CAS at the Rodgers Library: a pilot programme', *OCLC Systems and Services* 14(2): 71–7.

Gustitus, C. (1998) 'The push is on: what push technology means to the special librarian', *Information Outlook* 2(1): 21–4.

Hamilton, F. (1995) *Current Awareness, Current Techniques.* Aldershot: Gower.

Hammond, T., Hannay, T. and Lund, B. (2004) 'The role of RSS in science publishing', *D-Lib Magazine* 10(12); available at: *http://www.dlib.org/dlib/december04/hammond/12hammond.html* (accessed: 8 April 2006).

Hanka, R. and Fuka, K. (2000) 'Information overload and 'just-in-time' knowledge', *The Electronic Library* 18(4): 279–84.

Hanson, T. and Cox, J. A. (1993) 'Comparative review of two diskette-based current awareness services: current contents on diskette and reference update', *Database* 16(3): 73–81.

Haynes, M. E. (1987) *Personal Time Management.* Menlo Park, CA: CRISP Publications.

Heinström, J. (2003) 'Five personality dimensions and their influence on information behaviour', *Information Research* 9(1) paper 165; available at: *http://InformationR.net/ir/9-1/paper165.html* (accessed: 26 April 2006).

Hentz, M. B. (1996) 'Comparison and utilization of electronic table of contents delivery in a corporate library environment', *Journal of Interlibrary Loan, Document Delivery and Information Supply* 7(2): 29–41.

Holmes, G., McElwee, G. and Thomas, R. (1995)

'Environmental scanning and the information-gathering behaviour of headteachers', *International Journal of Educational Management* 9(5): 27–30.

Hopson, B. and Scally, M. (1993) *Time Management: Conquering the Clock*. Amsterdam: Pfeiffer.

Housman, E. M. (1973) 'Selective dissemination of information', *Annual Review of Information Science and Technology*, vol. 8: 221–41.

Hyams, E. (2005) 'Welcome', *CILIP Update* 4(11): 1.

Ingwersen, P. (1992) *Information Retrieval Interaction*. London: Taylor Graham.

Ingwersen, P. and Jarvelin, K. (2005) *The Turn: Integration of Information Seeking and Retrieval in Context*. Dordrecht: Springer.

Jansen, B. J. and Pooch, U. (2001) 'A review of web searching studies and a framework for future research', *Journal of the American Society for Information Science and Technology* 52(3): 235–246.

Jones, W. (2004) 'Finders, keepers? The present and future perfect in support of personal information management' *First Monday* 9(3); available at: *http://www.firstmondayorg/issues/issue9_3/jones/index.html* (accessed: 8 March 2006).

Karim, N. S. A. (2004) 'The link between environmental scanning (ES) and organizational information behavior: implications for research and the role of information professionals', *Library Review* 53(7): 356–62.

Kelly, W. E. (2003) 'No time to worry: the relationship between worry, time structure, and time management', *Personality and Individual Differences* 35: 1119–26.

Kemp, A. (1979) *Current Awareness Services*. London: Bingley.

Kim, K-S. and Allen, B. (2002) 'Cognitive and task influences on Web searching behavior', *Journal of the American*

Society for Information Science and Technology 53(2): 109–19.

Kirschner, P. A. (2002) 'Cognitive load theory: implications of cognitive load theory on the design of learning', *Learning and Instruction* 12(1): 1–10.

Klingerer, A. (1997) 'NewsNet smart-mail: push delivery gets smart', *Online* 21(5): 46–47.

Kuhlthau, C. C. (1991) 'Inside the search process: information seeking from the users' perspective', *Journal of the American Society for Information Science* 42(5): 361–71.

Kuhlthau, C. C. (1994) *Seeking Meaning: A Process Approach to Library and Information Services*. Norwood, NJ: Ablex,

Kuhlthau, C. C. (2004) *Seeking Meaning: A Process Approach to Library and Information Services* (2nd edn). Westpoint, CT: Libraries Unlimited.

Landau, H. B. (1969) 'Document dissemination', *Annual Review of Information Science and Technology*: 229–70.

Large, A., Beheshti, J. and Rahman, T. (2002) 'Gender differences in collaborative Web searching behavior: an elementary school study', *Information Processing and Management* 38: 427–43.

Lazonder, A. W., Biemans, H. J. A. and Wopereis, I. G. J. H. (2000) 'Differences between novice and experienced users in searching information on the World Wide Web', *Journal of the American Society for Information Science* 51(6): 576–81.

Limberg, L. (1999) 'Experiencing information seeking and learning: a study of the interaction between two phenomena', *Information Research* 5(1); available at: *http://informationr.net/ir/5-1/paper68.html* (accessed: 26 April 2006).

Makulowich, J. S. (1997) 'Alert and news services (on the Internet)', *Online* 21 (March): 82–4.

Mancini, M. (1994) *Time Management*. Burr Ridge, IL: Irwin/Mirror Press.

Martin, P. and Metcalfe, M. (2001) 'Informing the knowledge workers: principles of current awareness services', *Reference Services Review* 29(4): 267–75.

Merriam-Webster Online. Available at: *http://www.m-w.com/dictionary/alert* (accessed: 1 March 2006).

Mezzy, M. (2004) 'A reflective librarian's bookshelf', *CILIP Update* 3(7/8): 38–45.

Miller, R. (2004) 'Can RSS relieve information overload', *EContent* 27(3): 20–4.

Miller, S. M. (1987) 'Monitoring and blunting: validation of a questionnaire to assess styles of information seeking under threat', *Journal of Personality and Social Psychology* 52(2): 345–53.

Mort, D. (2005/2006). Industry considers RSS', *Research Information*, December 2005/January 2006: 20–1.

Mountifield, H. M. (1995) 'Electronic current awareness service: a survival tool for the information age?' *The Electronic Library* 13(4): 317–20.

Mulvany, T. (2000) *UKOLUG Quick Guide to Personal Bibliographic Software*. London: UK Online User Group.

Nahl, D. (2005) 'Affective load', in K. E. Fisher, S. Erdelez and L. McKechnie (eds) *Theories of Information Behavior*. Medford, NJ: Information Today; pp. 39–43.

Nesbeitt, S. L. and Gordon, R. S. (2002) *The Information Professional's Guide to Career Development Online*. Medford, NJ: Information Today.

Nicholas, D. and Dobrowolski, T. (1999) 'The tail wags the dog: the future of information is now', in A. Scammell (ed.) *I in the Sky: Visions of the Information Future*. London: Aslib: pp. 227–33.

OCLC (2003) 'Environmental scan: pattern recognition'; available at: *http://www.oclcorg/reports/escan/* (accessed: 26 April 2006).

OCLC (2005) 'OCLC perceptions of libraries and information resources'; available at: *http://www.oclcorg/reports/2005perceptions.htm* (accessed: 26 April 2006).

Ojala, M. (1997) 'The personality characteristics of newswires', *Database* 20(2): 14–26.

Palmer, J. (2004) 'A healthy profession?' *CILIP Update* 3(12): 32–3.

Pashiardis, P. (1996) 'Environmental scanning in educational organizations: uses, approaches, sources and methodologies', *International Journal of Educational Management* 10(3): 5–9.

Pedley, P. (2004) 'Have you thought of blogging?' *Update* 3(5): 32–3.

Pennanen, M. and Vakkari, P. (2002) 'Student's cognition and information searching while preparing a research proposal', in H. Bruce, R. Fidel, P. Ingwersen and P. Vakkarao (eds), *Proceedings of the 4th International Conference on Conceptions of Library and Information Science: Emerging Frameworks and Methods*, 21–25 July 2002. Greenwood Village, CO: Libraries Unlimited; pp. 33–48.

Phillips, N. (1997) *Reality Hacking*. Oxford: Capstone Publishing.

Prytherch, R. (1995) *Harrod's Librarians Glossary: 9000 Terms used in Information Management, Library Science, Publishing, the Book Trades, and Archive Management.* (8th edn). Aldershot: Gower.

Quint, B. (2005) 'Searcher's voice: the elusive un-client', *Searcher Magazine* 13(7); available at *http://www.Infotoday.com/SEARCHER/Jul05/voice.stml* (accessed: 16 June 2006).

Quiroga, L. M. and Mostafa, J. (2002) 'An experiment in building profiles in information filtering: the role of context of user relevance feedback', *Information Processing and Management* 38: 671–94.

Richards, D. (1992) 'Dissemination of information', in *Handbook of Special Librarianship and Information Work*. 6th edn. London: Aslib.

Rouse, W. B. and Rouse, S. H. (1984) 'Human information seeking and design of information systems', *Information Processing and Management* 20(1/2): 129–38.

Rowley, J. (1985) 'Bibliographic current awareness services: a review', *Aslib Proceedings* 37(9): 345–53.

Rowley, J. (1994) 'Revolution in current awareness services', *Journal of Librarianship and Information Science* 26(1): 7–14.

Rowley, J. (1998) 'Current awareness in an electronic age: *Online and CD-ROM Review* 22(4): 277–9.

Savolainen, R. (1995) 'Everyday life information seeking: approaching information seeking in the context of way of life'. *Library and Information Science Research* 17: 259–84.

Schamber, L. (2000) 'Time-line interviews and inductive content analysis: their effectiveness for exploring cognitive behaviors', *Journal of the American Society for Information Science* 51(8): 734–44.

Schuff, D., Turetken, O. and D'Arcy, J. (2005) 'A multi-attribute, multi-weight clustering approach to managing "e-mail overload"', *Decision Support Systems*. (Corrected proofread copy; volume and page numbers not available).

Shapira, B., Shoval, P. and Hanani, U. (1999) 'Experimentation with an information filtering system that combines cognitive and sociological filtering integrated with user stereotypes', *Decision Support Systems* 27: 5–24.

Simpson, C. W. and Prusak, L. (1995) 'Troubles with information overload – moving from quantity to quality in information provision', *International Journal of Information Management* 15(6): 413–25.

Slaughter, R. A. (1999) 'A new framework for environmental scanning', *Foresight* 1(5): 441–51.

Smith, D. (1999) *Work With What You Have: Ways to Creative and Meaningful Livelihood*. Boston: Shambhala.

Spink, A. (1997) 'Study of interactive feedback during mediated information retrieval', *Journal of the American Society for Information Science* 48(5): 382–94.

Spink, A., Bateman, J. and Greisdorf, H. (1999) 'Successive searching behaviour during information seeking: an exploratory study', *Journal of Information Science* 25: 439–49.

Stenstrom, P. F. and Tegler, P. (1988) 'Current awareness in librarianship', *Library Trends* 36(4): 725–40.

Sullivan, P. (2004) 'Information overload: keeping current without being overwhelmed', *Science and Technology* 25(1/2): 109–25.

Taylor, R. (1986) 'Question-negotiation and information seeking in libraries', *College and Research Libraries* 29(3): 178–94.

Tedd, L. A. and Yeates, R. (1998) 'A personalized current awareness service for library and information services staff: an overview of the NewsAgent for libraries project', *Program* 32(4): 373–90.

Todd, R. J. (2005) 'Information intents', in K. E. Fisher, S. Erdelez and L. McKechnie (eds) *Theories of Information Behavior*. Medford, NJ: Information Today; pp. 198–203.

Trench, S. (1997) 'Dissemination of information', in A. Scammel (ed.) *Handbook of Special Librarianship and Information Work*. London: Aslib.

Vakkari, P. (1998) 'Growth of theories on information seeking: an analysis of growth of a theoretical research program on the relation between task complexity and information seeking', *Information Processing and Management* 34(2/3): 361–82.

Vakkari, P. (1999) 'Task complexity, problem structure and information actions: integrating studies on information seeking and retrieval', *Information Processing and Management* 35: 819–37.

Vakkari, P. (2001) 'A theory of the task-based information retrieval process: a summary and generalization of a longitudinal study', *Journal of Documentation* 57(1): 44–60.

Vakkari, P. (2003) 'Task-based information searching', *Annual Review of Information Science and Technology* 37: 413–64.

Van Brakel, P. A. and Potgieter, H. C. (1997) 'Creating World-Wide Web bulletin boards to enhance current awareness services', *South African Journal of Library and Information Science* 65(2): 124–9.

Voros, J. (2001) 'Reframing environmental scanning: an integral approach. *Foresight* 3(6): 533–51.

Waldman, M. (2003) 'Freshmen's use of library electronic resources and self-efficacy', *Information Research* 8(2); available at: *http://informationr.net/ir/8-2/paper150.html* (accessed: 26 April 2006).

Wei, C-P. and Lee, Y-H. (2004) 'Event detection from online news documents for supporting environmental scanning', *Decision Support Systems* 36: 385–401.

Wente, V. A. and Young, G. A. (1970) 'Current awareness and dissemination', *Annual Review of Information Science and Technology* 5. Medford, NJ: Information Today; pp. 259–95.

Whitehall, T. (1982) 'Dissemination of information', in L. J. Anthony (ed.) *Handbook of Special Librarianship and Information Work* (8th edn). London: Aslib; pp. 355–73.

Whitehall, T. (1985) 'Current awareness in education: an evaluation of Trent Polytechnic's education news', *Aslib Proceedings* 37: 355–70.

Williams, M. (1978) 'Online retrieval: today and tomorrow'. *Online Review* 24(4): 353–66.

Williams, R. V. (1988) 'Productivity measures in special libraries: prospects and problems for use in performance evaluation', *Special Libraries* 79(2): 101–14.

Wilson, K. and Strouse, R. (2005) 'Learning from peers: benchmarking your information managing activities', *Information Outlook* 9(9): 25–6, 29–31.

Wilson, P. (1993) 'The value of currency', *Library Trends* 41(4): 362–73.

Wilson, T. D. (1981) 'On user studies and information needs', *Journal of Librarianship* 37(1): 3–15; available at: *http://informationr.net/tdw/publ/papers/1981infoneeds.html* (accessed: 25 April 2006).

Wilson, T. D. (1999a) 'Exploring models of information behaviour: the 'uncertainty' project', *Information Processing and Management* 35: 839–49.

Wilson, T. D. (1999b) 'Models in information behaviour research', *Journal of Documentation* 55(3): 249–70.

Wilson, T. D., Ford, N. J., Ellis, D., Foster, A. E. and Spink, A. (2002) 'Information seeking and mediated searching. Part 2: uncertainty and its correlates', *Journal of the American Society for Information Science and Technology* 53(9): 704–15.

Winship, I. (2004) 'Weblogs and RSS in information work', *Update* 3(5): 30–1.

Woodburn, H. M. (1972) 'Retrieval and use of the literature of inorganic chemistry', *Journal of Chemical Education* 49(10): 689–96.

Yeates, R. (1999) 'Have you heard the library news? Personalized net alert for librarians', *Aslib Proceedings* 51(5): 137–42.

Yep, D. S. M. (1994) *Creativity at Work: Business Skills Express Series*. Burr Ridge, IL: Irwin.

Zick, L. (2000) 'The work of information mediators: a comparison of librarians and intelligent software agents', *First Monday* 5(5); available at: *http://firstmondayorg/ issues/issue5_5/zick/index.html* (accessed: 8 March 2006).

Index

Only examples of alerting services of specific importance or which are described in more detail are indexed individually. All other examples are listed in the Appendix.

CAS is an abbreviation for 'current awareness services', LIS for 'library and information service' and SDI for 'selective dissemination of information'.